How to Write a PICTURE BOOK

Tips & Tricks For Writing Illustrated Picture Books for Kids

Darcy Pattison

Mims House | Little Rock, AR

Mims House
www.mimshouse.com
1309 Broadway
Little Rock, AR 72202

ISBN: 978-0-9798621-6-8 (eBook)
ISBN: 978-0-9852134-8-0 (paperback)

TABLE OF CONTENTS

PICTURE BOOKS

Children's literature includes a special category of books, illustrated books that appeal to kids. These are designed to give children something to look at while they listen to or read a story. The genre has developed over the last 100 years into a unique art and literary form. This book will talk about the genre from many angles, including the characteristics unique to picture books, how eBooks are changing the genre, sub-genres of pictures books, and how to write and submit picture books for publication. If you want to really understand picture books, be sure to take the time to read the suggested titles. Look out—you may get hooked on this deceptively simple book genre.

HOW TO USE THIS BOOK

Are you ready to jump into writing a picture book? Before you start writing, take this quiz:

1. How many pages are in a typical children's picture book?
2. Who is the audience for a children's picture book?
3. Are there restrictions on the vocabulary you use in a picture book?
4. Do you have to write in rhyme? Do manuscripts written in rhyme sell better?
5. Do ePub books have to be the same length as printed books?

If you know the answers to most of these questions, you're ready to write! If you're not sure about a couple, then review the Picture Book Basics.

YOU CAN TAKE ONE OF THREE ROUTES THROUGH THIS BOOK

If you are comfortable that you know the basics of picture books, then it's time to move to the next two sections of the book, Genres and Write. You can use one of these strategies to write, revise and submit your story:

1. Read about specific genres first and then the specific steps of writing and revising a picture book. Go to the Workbook section and write.

2. Read about writing and revising a picture book; read only the genre specifics you need for your type of picture book. Go to the Workbook section and write.

3. A combination of the first two options. You could read a couple genres while studying how to write a picture book, and then, read a couple more genres as you decide on the topic for your story. Go to the Workbook section and write.

BASICS

Let's get started! Here, we'll discuss some of the basics of picture books. In each lesson, I mention specific picture books titles to make a point. You should try to find these books at your library and read through each. At the end of each lesson, try to find ten more books that illustrate the point. It's best to use books published within the last five years because this will help you become familiar with what is being published today. Here are the topics we'll discuss:

Picture Book Structure: Why 32 Pages?
Does ePub Change the 32-page Illustrated Picture Book?
Putting the Picture in Picture Books
The Dual Audience for Picture Books
Picture Book Settings
Options for Picture Book Characters
Messages, Morals and Lessons in Picture Books
Picture Books: Folk Tales or Modern Stories?
General Resources for Picture Books

PICTURE BOOK STRUCTURE: WHY 32 PAGES?

Let's start with the most noticeable difference about children's picture books: they are short. Picture books are almost always 32 pages. The reasons for this are physical: when you fold paper, eight pages fold smoothly into what's called a signature. Any more pages results in a group of pages too thick to bind nicely. In addition, the 32 pages can all be printed on a single sheet of paper, making it cost-effective. In extremely rare cases, picture books may be 16, 24, 40 or 48 pages, all multiples of eight (a signature); but 32 pages is industry standard.

Francoise Bui of Doubleday Books says, "We'll do a longer book if the story needs it. The most likely time is if it's a holiday or seasonal book, that we plan to give a bigger marketing push, and it needs those extra pages to tell the story. If I've acquired a story I really like, and if it needs extra pages, I'll do it."

There are variations: in my picture book, *The Journey of Oliver K. Woodman*, the illustrator, Joe Cepeda, takes 48 pages to tell the story. The text is letters or postcards, written by someone who gives a lift to Oliver, a wooden man, who then writes back to Uncle Ray to report on Oliver's progress across the nation from South Carolina to California. There are fourteen letters for fourteen spreads. Cepeda added wordless spreads between each letter to show Oliver actually traveling. It gives the book a more spacious feel, as if the reader is traveling along with Oliver. So, you may see board books at 16 or 24 pages, and picture books at 32, 40 or 48 pages. But the gold standard for picture books is 32 pages.

PICTURE BOOK LAYOUTS

When you lay out pages for a picture book story, there are two options. First, you can look at each page separately. Second, you can talk about double-page spreads; when a picture book is opened flat, the two facing pages are often illustrated as one. Thus, in a 32-page book, you would have a single opening page (the right hand side of the book), fifteen double-page spreads, and a single closing page (the left hand side of the book). Decorative end papers may be glued to the cover boards, which would enclose them. Sometimes, the end papers are counted as part of the 32 pages, and sometimes they are not. If you see a picture book that says it has 28 pages, the end papers make up part of the signature.

In those 32 pages, there are usually "front matter" pages consisting of a title page, a half-title page, and a copyright page. Sometimes, there's a dedication page. In single pages, this may take 4-5 pages. In double-page spreads, it's the first single page and one or two spreads. The text then has 27-28 pages or 14 spreads, plus a last single page.

Many conventions have grown up around the 32-page picture book: the page 32 twist, the character opening, the use of double-page spreads, and so on, all things we'll get to later. All that is good. Writers and illustrators took the restricted format and made it into a thing of beauty.

One way to visualize the picture book layout is by using the thumbnail layout (See the Thumbnail Layout in the Workbook section.) The layout shows a small version of how a book fits into 32 pages. It's called a thumbnail because the illustrator does a rapid sketch, thumbnail size, to illustrate the layout. The X before page 1 and after page 32 means that these pages do not exist.

SHORT STORY OR PICTURE BOOK?

Concentrating on the skeleton of the picture book may seem boring or unnecessary, but it is one of the two main differences between short stories and picture books. One mistake made by beginners is to have too many or too few pages to fit into this format. Why can't the publisher ignore the standard page limits and just print the size book needed for a particular story? Again, the reasons are physical: the way the paper folds and standard sizes of paper for printing. Literary agent Tracey Adams says, "It's definitely easiest to market a picture book meant to be the standard 32 pages."

QUESTION: 32 PAGES? PLEASE EXPLAIN MORE

Question: It isn't clear to me the relationship between the pages of a picture book and the pages of typed text that the author writes. Does an author just write text and the publisher divides it into 32 pages? Or should the author divide the text and show the page breaks when submitting the manuscript.

Answer: There's a big difference between book length and manuscript length. 32 pages of finished book equals five (or fewer) pages of typed, double-spaced manuscript text, or in the range of 0-1000 words. And shorter is better.

Don't Show Page Breaks. When you send in the manuscript to a publisher, you send it in standard manuscript format (five pages or so). When the text is laid out for the picture book, the editor, art director and illustrator will divide it into the segments that go on each page.

You should divide your text into 14-28 segments, anticipating how it will be laid out in a picture book. However, that is strictly to help you, the author, revise and polish the text. When you send in the manuscript, it should be in standard manuscript format.

ACTION POINTS

Count pages. Visit a library or bookstore and go through 10 picture books counting pages. You'll find some variety, which comes from whether or not the end papers are counted as pages or not. Count pages in some board books (the cardboard books for babies and toddlers); this will vary widely because board books are not printed and produced the same as picture books. How often do you find picture books longer than 32 pages?

Type up a manuscript. Choose a favorite published children's book and type it up as a manuscript in standard manuscript format: 1" margins, 12 pt Times New Roman, double-spaced, and each page is numbered. Typing it in this standard format will help you visualize the difference between a manuscript and a published book.

On the next two pages, you'll see two manuscript pages of my book, *Rowdy: The Pirate Who Could Not Sleep*. It's shrunken some to fit the size of this book, but it should give you a good idea of how a manuscript looks when formatted to the simple standard.

Darcy Pattison
Add Contact Info
Address
eMail Address

408 words

Include full contact information so an editor can respond.

Word count belongs in upper right hand corner.

ROWDY: The Pirate Who Could Not Sleep

by

Darcy Pattison

Title and author are listed about halfway down page one.

Yo, ho!

Miss Whitney Black McKee

Was Cap'n of a sleek hulled sloop

And a rowdy pirate was she.

"I have not slept since we left Shanghai,

With a monster in our wake.

We fought it o'er the miles of waves.

Me heart and hands still ache."

Number every page. If the manuscript is accidentally dropped, the editor can easily put them aback in order.

1

The wide-eyed Captain lamented,

"Me sleep's gone all awry

I'd give a chest of me finest gold

For a simple lullaby."

The crewmen set their feet ashore.

Those scalawags went a'thievin'.

They crouched and peered through cracks in doors,

And scowled at mothers a'singin'.

"But how do thieves thieve a lullaby?"

They puzzled through the twilight.

"How do you steal what can't be held?"

They puzzled through the night.

The cabin boy stole the Cap'n's log,

And read of haunted dreams

And secrets that the Cap'n kept.

Then—he searched up quiet streams.

The first mate stole a music box

Double space throughout. Here, I used a double-double space to show stanzas of the poem. But you should usually indent to show paragraphs.

PICTURE BOOK ILLUSTRATIONS

Picture books are illustrated stories. What does that mean to the writer of the picture book text?

The biggest difference between short stories and picture books is the illustrations. Magazine stories, for example, may have one or two illustration possibilities. Picture books, however, have an illustration possibility on each page. You must think visually when writing for this genre.

Thinking visually doesn't mean adjectives; illustrators can fill in colors, background, clothing, and other details. Instead, concentrate on verbs. Telling a compelling picture book story requires action. Unless a description is crucial to the story, cut it. Only include actions that move the story along. Thoughts and dialogue may advance the plot, but they can't be illustrated; talking heads make for boring illustrations. Picture book stories find ways to make thoughts concrete in exciting ways.

Think of it this way: the poor illustrator only get the visual details, but you get everything else, including hearing, feeling, tasting, smelling and moving in space. Only include the visual details in the text if it really makes a difference to the story; otherwise, leave it to the illustrator.

VISUAL POSSIBILITIES

In other words, you are providing visual possibilities, not visual directions. You will give the illustrator one or two choices for each double-page spread; however, the final choice belongs to the illustrator.

Be careful, though, about what illustration possibilities you provide. In my picture book, *The Journey of Oliver K. Woodman,* I had the characters visit Reno, Nevada, where they attend a rodeo, visit a casino and win $5000! I assumed that the illustrator would illustrate the rodeo.

17

In fact, I wanted that rodeo illustration. I grew up hearing my Dad announce rodeos, and I especially remember how he called the barrel rides: "A pretty ride by a pretty little lady."

Instead, the illustration for that text shows Agnes, Maggie and Lucinda—and Oliver K. Woodman—at a gambling table. Joe Cepeda did an amazing illustration, but not what I really wanted! In the sequel, *Searching for Oliver K. Woodman*, I send the wooden woman, the P.I. searching for Oliver, to another rodeo. This time there was no other illustration possibility: I got my rodeo scene.

If you provide illustrators with several illustration possibilities, it's up to them to choose what to illustrate.

ACTION POINTS

Study relationship between art and text. Choose about five picture books and study each page. Think about why the illustrator chose the content of the art. Did the text demand something specific, or did the illustrator exercise freedom in the illustrations and add something extra?

The Irma Simonton Black and James H. Black Award for Excellence in Children's Literature (Irma Black Award), sponsored by the Bank Street College, goes to an outstanding book for young children - a book in which text and illustrations are inseparable, each enhancing and enlarging on the other to produce a singular whole. Children judge the final selections.

Look at the list of previous winners and try to identify how the text and art work together. If you changed one or the other, what would happen to the story?

Find more information and a list of past winners at this website:
https://www.bankstreet.edu/center-childrens-literature/irma-black-award/

STUDY PICTURE BOOK AWARDS

There are several major awards for children's picture books. This list isn't exhaustive, but it includes the major U.S. national awards. Many states also have award programs, often voted on by the students/children of that state. Other countries have children's book awards, also, so look for those. Study the award-winning books to see the best of current children's literature. Each award has a slightly different focus, which means it's a great way to study that aspect of children's books.

Randolph Caldecott Medal – Awarded by the American Library Association to the illustrator of the most distinguished American picture book for children.
(http://www.ala.org/alsc/awardsgrants/bookmedia/caldecottmedal/caldecottmedal)

Irma Simonton Black and James H. Black Award for Excellence in Children's Literature – Given by Bank Street College to an outstanding book for young children – a book in which text and illustrations are inseparable, each enhancing and enlarging on the other to produce a singular whole. (https://www.bankstreet.edu/center-childrens-literature/irma-black-award/)

Cook Prize – The Cook Prize, given by the Bank Street College, honors the best science, technology, engineering and math (STEM) picture book published for children aged eight to ten. It is the only national children's choice award honoring a STEM book. (Nonfiction)
(https://www.bankstreet.edu/center-childrens-literature/cook-prize/)

Margaret Wise Brown Prize for Children's Literature – Given by Hollins University to the best picture book text.

(https://www.hollins.edu/academics/graduate-degrees/childrens-literature-graduate-program/margaret-wise-brown-prize-childrens-literature/)

E.B. White Read Aloud award – Given by the ABC Group of the American Bookseller's Association for the best read aloud books. (https://theabfc.wordpress.com/the-eb-white-read-aloud-awards/)

Hans Christian Andersen Award – International award from the International Board on Books for Young People (IBBY) for "lasting contribution to literature for children and young people." (www.ibby.org)

Boston Globe-Horn Book Award – Given by the Horn Book Magazine and the Boston Globe newspaper for high quality and overall creative excellence. (www.hbook.com/bghb/)

Children's Book Guild Award for Nonfiction – Goes to an author for a body of work that has "contributed significantly to the quality of nonfiction for children." (www.childrensbookguild.org)

Golden Kite Awards – From the Society of Children's Bookwriters and Illustrators are given for both picture book illustrations and picture book text. (www.scbwi.org)

Coretta Scott King Book Awards – Given by the American Library Association for book celebrating the African American experience. (www.ala.org/csk)

Orbis Pictus Award for Outstanding Nonfiction for Children – From the National Council of Teachers of English (www.ncte.org/awards/orbispictus)

ACTION POINTS

If you could choose just one of the awards above, which would you want? Would you rather have a great read aloud book or an outstanding nonfiction book? Choose a couple awards and read the recent winners. Do you still aspire to that award?

THE CASE OF PRINT ON DEMAND (POD)

I recently watched *Miss Potter*, the movie based on the life of children's book author and illustrator Beatrix Potter. It's a fascinating look at the life of one of the all-time best selling authors of children's books. When my children were small, I read *The Tale of Peter Rabbit* to them so many times that I've memorized it.

One line in the movie caught my interest. When the publishing company was first discussing her book, Beatrix had definite opinions on how it should be published: black and white illustrations so that the price could be kept low. However, the publisher had another idea on how to keep the price low. If the book's color interior pages could all be printed on a single sheet of paper, it would be economical and the price could be kept at an attractive low price.

That decision–to design the book for an economical printing model–was genius and partly responsible for the huge popularity of *The Tale of Peter Rabbit*. That model is so popular that today that children's picture books that are offset printed are still designed for printing the whole book on one sheet of paper. 32-page picture books are the standard in the industry, not because it's the best length for a story, but because the printing was economical. However, because that length became a standard, there's now, more or less, a standard type story told in children's picture books.

But the question for today is this: what is the most economical way to produce a children's illustrated story given today's technology options? That answer varies because of print-on-demand and eBook technologies. Print-on-demand (POD) means that your book is stored digitally on a printing company's computers. When a book is ordered, the book is printed, bound and delivered. This eliminates the need for warehousing, and it has the advantage of bundling the fulfillment (mailing the book) with the printing. Instead of buying 1000 copies of a book, publishers/authors/self-publishers can set up a book with a POD company with very little up-front investment. It's perfect for the self-publisher or small publisher who doesn't want to invest a lot in stock.

However, POD's biggest disadvantage is price. Because you print one book at a time, the unit cost is often two or three times that of offset printing. This is usually fine because selling online eliminates the extra cost of whole-saling to a bookstore.

POD also means that the 32-page picture book is no longer mandatory. For example, Amazon's Createspace.com or LightningSpark.com require a minimum of 24-pages, but after that you can add as many or as few pages as you like. 26 pages? That's fine for a POD printer.

Likewise, digital ebooks can be any length you want. Two pages? Well, most of us wouldn't call that a book! But if you can make the case for it, it is possible.

The 32-page illustrated picture book made sense for years because the offset printing presses could accommodate huge sheets of paper holding 32 pages exactly. The process made sense economically.

Today, these are your options.

Offset printing: With this traditional printing method, you'll get much lower unit costs if you stick to the 32-page standard book.

POD printing: You accept higher per-unit costs because you don't have to warehouse. The length is up to you.

eBook: You accept that this is only delivered and read digitally. Page length is variable.

I still design my books for 32-pages because I do both print and eBooks and because I've learned to write to that length. But also, it leaves me open to short-run offset printing for special orders where it makes sense to go for a smaller per unit cost. By sticking with the industry standards, I have even more options.

ACTION POINTS

If you plan to indie, or self-publish, think about how you will publish your books. Will you do both print and digital books? If so, how will you handle the issue of how many pages in your picture books?

THE CASE OF EPUB, OR EBOOKS

As we said, POD and digital publishing blow apart the 32-page standard. Let's look at ebooks in more detail. There are two ways to publish a picture book digitally. First, you might make it into an app for use on electronic devices, but especially an iTunes or Android app. Second, the book can become an ePub. ePub (http://idpf.org/ePub) is the standard for displaying information in a digital book format. Basically, it uses a form of html (hypertext mark-up language) that is used to code webpages, allows for CSS (cascading style sheets), which controls how the information looks, and adds a container for all the files. The rest of what I'll say here refers to ePub, not apps.

In contrast to printing a book, ePub doesn't deal with paper or printing presses. One way to think about an ePub is that it is one long, continuous webpage. It happens to be displayed one "page" at a time on an eBook reader, but the person reading can change the type font used and font size, which means each person's page can look unique. When an ePub has text that can easily change size, it's called reflowable text, or text that will expand or shrink depending on the setting of the eBook reader.

One problem with this is that each eBook reader displays the book differently. An ePub will look slightly different depending on the reader used. You can develop some consistency by tweaking the book's code for each platform of Kindle, Nook, iBook, Kobo, or other readers, but it's never exactly the same from reader to reader.

ePub presents a problem for an illustrated picture book: how do you keep the text and images together if everything is reflowable? It's not easy. When you try to keep the image and text together, it's called a fixed format ePub. For these, the book's code won't allow text to reflow to the next page by itself.

Instead, it keeps the images and text together on a page. This is accomplished in one of two ways.

First, you can embed the text in the image, which makes the eBook a series of images. This allows simple control of where the text is displayed because it's on the image. The images also make for a simple production process. It's almost like making a pdf file of the story, except each page is a separate file saved in an image format for ePub display. I consider this the lowest common denominator and the most likely to display well across platforms. However, this format loses some advantages of ebooks, such as the ability to search text. Using images to create an ePub is a trade-off, but one I often take to ensure the widest compatibility.

Second, you can use CSS to control the display of the images and text. This is more difficult because it requires some knowledge of html and CSS, along with the idiosyncrasies of each ebook platform. With each new iteration of an ereader, it becomes more difficult. Right now, if you count all the ereaders and then add in new generations of each, you might need to format for over 70 different devices. It's a daunting task and there are bound to be problems.

This type of ePub can imitate the double-page spreads of print books, but it's not universally supported across ereaders. Without a fixed layout, you are limited to single images in the portrait orientation. With fixed layouts on some devices, you can force the display to turn landscape and show two pages side-by-side.

For those who prefer to do it manually, and thus gain exact control of the layout, recommended software includes Jutoh, Calibre, Sigil, Scrivener, and other eBook creation platforms. R. Scot Johns maintains an excellent tutorial on creating fixed format ePubs on his Fantasy Castle site: http://www.fantasycastlebooks.com/Tutorials/ibooks-tutorial-part1.html. He also keeps updated on the changing needs of new Kindle formats and does consulting on projects.

To make creating a fixed-format ePub accessible to most people, in September, 2014, Amazon released software for creating fixed format books, the free Kindle Kids Book Creator program. (https://kdp.amazon.com/kids). Apple also has free software to create fixed format ebooks, the iBooks Author app (http://www.apple.com/ibooks-author/). Through these programs, most people can easily format a fixed format ePub.

Which brings us back to our question: do ePub picture books need to be 32 pages?

Short answer: No. ePub illustrated books for children can be any length you want.

However, the real question is whether you want to only do an ePub, or if you are also interested in a print version. If you want a paperback or hardcover book, you may want to stick with the industry standard of 32 pages because it will be easier to move it to POD or a commercial printing press.

32 pages? Yes, if you want the best prices on a printed quantity of books. Or, if you think at some point you might want to print. So far, traditional publishers are sticking to the 32 pages because it is the most economical.

32 pages? No, if you only want to use ePub and POD. 24 pages is the minimum for POD, but you can do whatever size you want after that.

In my mind, an apt analogy is poetry, which was bound for years by strict forms like a sonnet. When free verse swept through the poetry world, it resulted in amazing creativity and wonderful poetry. Those who still favored sonnets were still writing great poetry, and to attempt a sonnet is still a wonderful thing. But free verse allowed for a different sort of expression, a different sort of verse. It meant redefining what poetry was and is. I think we are at the threshold of doing the same thing for children's illustrated picture books. The form no longer restricts anything; but that puts more of a burden on the creativity of the author and book designer on how to use the freer format to its best advantage in telling a great story or sharing great information.

ACTION POINTS

Look at and read some children's illustrated eBooks. Read about POD printing. Investigate the app market, as well, the other option for a children's illustrated picture book. One popular app is EPIC!, a subscription based service which allows access to 14,000 ebooks.

Decide what format you want to write for and adapt everything in this book to that format.

THE DUAL AUDIENCE

Who is the real audience for a children's picture book? Parents or kids?

THE CHILD AS AUDIENCE

When you write a picture book, you must remember that the audience is a child, so the story should be of interest to them. Unless it is a folk or fairy tale, characters are usually children. Rarely do adult characters or inanimate objects as characters make successful picture books.

Yes, I know about SpongeBob and Veggie Tales. But those stories really shouldn't work. Really? A talking tomato? A sponge with an attitude? Only the most skilled writers can pull this off and usually not in a picture book. It takes video, with its moving features and accompanying voice, to characterize inanimate things well.

Doubleday editor, Francoise Bui says, "It's preferable to have a young child as protagonist, or an animal. It needs to be someone who the child reader can relate to."

THE ADULT AS AUDIENCE

However, adults are the gatekeepers for children's access to picture books. For the youngest children, an adult reads to them and you must remember this as you write.

Australian writer Mem Fox says it's important to keep in mind "the child in the lap," in other words, the relationship between the adult and the child as you write the story. For example, include something that will make the child turn to the adult and give them a hug.

Can the adult stand to read your story 100 times? Favorite children's books are often requested over and over by a child, so you must consider if the adult can stand it "one more time." As you write, pay attention to how easily the words flow.

Adult have their own needs and uses for children's literature. Remember that often the adult is a teacher who uses picture books to fulfill something in the education curriculum. This shouldn't be the major concern, but if you can tie it into a curriculum need, it will help sell your picture book. For example, *The Journey of Oliver K. Woodman* is used in social studies for map work and in language arts to teach letter writing.

ACTION POINTS

Child in the Lap. Find five books that you consider perfect for the dual audience of adults and children. Try to find something for toddlers, preschoolers and school age kids. Look for places the author has built something into the story that will encourage a strong child-adult relationship. What are the differences as kids get older?

PICTURE BOOK SETTINGS: EXOTIC V. FAMILIAR

The setting of a picture book is important because it determines much of the illustrations.

When writing for kids, you walk a fine line between what is familiar v. exotic. Kids like the familiarity of neighborhoods, homes and schools. Yet, they also need to have their world expanded, and literature is a great way to do that. Try to stretch the setting, yet keep something familiar.

Where The Wild Things Are, by Maurice Sendak, starts at home, sends the character out for a fantastic visit, then brings him back to the comfort of home again.

Think of the Caldecott-Honor picture book, *King Bidgood's in the Bathtub*, by Audrey Wood, which uses the familiar ritual of a nightly bath, but turns it into something exotic.

Or, turn something exotic into something familiar, as in *Rachel and Obadiah*, by Brinton Turkle, which treats a Quaker family in a historical setting as the family-next-door.

SUGGESTED READING FOR FAMILIAR V. EXOTIC

Visit your local library or a bookstore and study the settings of children's picture books. Here are titles to get you started.

Familiar
School: *Officer Buckle and Gloria*, by Peggy Rathman
Outdoors: *My Friend Rabbit*, by Eric Rohmann

Exotic
Traveling across country: *The Journey of Oliver K. Woodman* by Darcy Pattison
Other countries: *The Diary of A Wombat* by Jackie French
Fantasy settings: *The Diary of a Worm* by Doreen Cronin

Combination of Familiar and Exotic
School and Imaginative Play: *19 Girls and Me* by Darcy Pattison
Animals interact with humans: *Diary of a Wombat* by Jackie French (wombat interacts with humans)

Please note that an exotic setting can't save a "weak" story, but it might give it an extra edge of uniqueness that helps it work better. Could *Diary of a Wombat* have been about a squirrel? No. And that's why the Australian setting works.

ACTION POINTS
Find five picture books, each with a unique setting. How is the setting established in the text, not just in the pictures? Imagine the story in a different setting: how would the change affect the story?

PICTURE BOOK CHARACTERS

Picture book characters can make or break the story. We usually think of kids, or at least humans, as the main characters, but there are other options.

EXAMPLES OF PICTURE BOOK CHARACTERS

Humans

10 Little Fingers, 10 Little Toes by Mem Fox. All the babies in this book are realistic babies.

Inanimate objects

Pumpkin Heads by Wendell Minor pictures a variety of pumpkins carved into jack-o-lanterns, and the story never really has a main character.

Little Blue and Little Yellow by Leo Lionni is illustrated with irregular blobs that represent family members. It's the ultimate in non-representational art.

Animals as Characters

There are two options here: are the characters really animals, or are they treated as humans in an animal skin?

1) Animals as Kids

The key is to observe children closely and make the animals act like humans.

My Friend Rabbit by Eric Rohmann features animals who act human.

2) Animals as Animals

Vulture View by April Pulley Sayre is a nonfiction picture book, with a literary bent, featuring vultures who really act as vultures.

Mixing Humans with either an Inanimate Objects or Animals
The Journey of Oliver K. Woodman by Darcy Pattison. A wooden man interacts with a variety of humans, who all treat him as a person.

Think about your options for characters and why you might want to use one or another in a story. How would the story of *My Friend, Rabbit* be different if the animals were acting as real animals?

SUPPORTING CHARACTERS

Besides the main character, your story likely needs supporting characters. Here are some concepts to keep in mind.

Use a variety of characters. Keep in mind that a wide cast of supporting characters adds to the story: family, school friends, best friends, bullies, etc.

Make characters, even supporting characters, stand out. Build in variety, contrasts, and conflicts by adding the right characters. Just be sure to keep characterizations under control so your main character isn't overwhelmed.

Limit the number of characters. For picture books, keep the total number of characters fairly small, but don't be afraid to stretch when the story demands it. Or find ways to keep the characters manageable; for example, in my story, *19 Girls and Me*, only a few of the 19 girls are actually named, but just including 19 girls creates the classroom atmosphere.

ACTION POINTS

This time, read picture books in search of unique main characters and supporting characters. Which ones appeal to you? Why? What kinds of contrasts do you find among the characters within one story?

MESSAGES, MORALS AND LESSONS

A novice writer wondered, "It seems there are many picture books with 'messages,' such as *Cowboy Camp* by Tammi Sauer, *Edwina the Dinosaur* by Mo Willems, and even *Sylvester and the Magic Pebble* by William Steig. And I've heard over and over that a writer shouldn't hit the reader over the head with a moral or message, so I'm wondering if there is an objective way of measuring didacticism in a picture book manuscript."

These are hard questions about writing a picture book. Some think that picture books are the perfect way to teach children a lesson. Others think picture books should only entertain. But literature, for adults or for children, crosses lines fluidly with important themes and ideas and entertainment that's funny or action-oriented. However, many object when children's books become too "preachy." Young audiences deserve the same respect as adult readers. If you wouldn't preach to adults, you shouldn't preach to kids.

Let's take a look at those preachy or didactic books.

How could you write the same message or moral in a story, but in a less preachy manner?

Are there any questions writers can ask themselves to ensure they aren't hitting the readers over the head with a lesson?

How do you show the main character's growth in the picture book without making the main character's lesson a blatant lesson for all who read the book?

Where is the line between too light a theme and too strong a message?

It is hard to balance teaching and entertainment. We want stories and picture books that kids want to read over and over. We don't want stories that adults think the kids need to read over and over. No one, especially kids, likes to be preached at.

WHAT'S THE PICTURE BOOK'S TAKEAWAY?

For me, it helps to change the question from, "What's the lesson?" to "What's the takeaway?"

After a picture book is read and done, what does the reader/listener take away from this story? That could be a moral or lesson, but it could be just a comforting feeling that it's safe to go to bed because there are no monsters under the bed. The range of successful takeaways can vary widely.

WRITING A STORY WITH A MESSAGE, MORAL OR LESSON

But what if you want to write a picture book to teach kids a lesson? You want them to share toys, or be kind to an elderly neighbor.

First, consider if the picture book is the right medium. Would this be better as a *Bible* study lesson, or as a curriculum lesson?

If you're sure that the picture book is the right medium, then keep these things in mind:

Picture Book Characters. Start with character, not the lesson. Start with a character who passionately wants something that s/he can't have, or fears something that must be faced. The struggles of a character — even a picture book character — are something that readers are willing to follow.

Picture Book Language and Voice. Next, make sure the language, the voice of the story, sings. Use every skill you know to build in great rhythm, evocative language, read-aloud qualities, etc. Build the plot carefully, page turn by page turn, keeping the tension high enough that it keeps the reader turning pages.

Show, don't tell. Unless you're Aesop, don't feel compelled to actually state the moral or lesson. Sometimes the strongest insights from reading come when the reader has the epiphany, even though it's not stated explicitly in the text.

SMART MARKETING FOR YOUR PICTURE BOOK

A last idea is to market smart. Some publishers are more likely to take a message-driven picture book than others. Most trade publishers (those which sell mostly to book stores) will shy away from this; instead, look to educational publishers, religious publishers and niche publishers. For example, for many years Albert Whitman published what they called "concept books," which to them meant stories about special needs children: diabetes, autism, dealing with death, deafness, etc. Almost by the nature of these books, they tended to be message-driven. Albert Whitman no longer publishes the concept books, but if you dig around, you'll find publishers who concentrate on your favorite niche topics for their publishing program. If you feel strongly that your picture book needs a certain moral, message or lesson, fine. Just strengthen every other aspect of the story, including character and voice. Then, market smart.

ACTION POINTS

Think about this question: should every children's book teach a moral? Are books for teaching or entertainment? Does it depend on the story or the market? There's no right or wrong answer, but just your opinion, which will help shape your career.

Search for examples of picture books that effectively teach a moral. Does the book also entertain? Search for one that entertains. Does it also teach a moral? Which do you aspire to write?

CHARACTERS: FOLK TALE OR MODERN STORY?

Despite writing and selling several children's picture books, I still receive many rejections. Why? That's what I recently set out to learn.

My search began with an article by Jill Paton Walsh, the grande dame of British children's literature. In an article in the *Horn Book Magazine* (January/February 2003, pages 21-27), she contrasted characters in folk tales and modern stories. Folk tales deal with characters in their family roles—mother, father, child, sibling. The stories themselves are often symbolic and defy rational analysis. The Billy Goats Gruff characters are just goats in a certain birth order, nothing more and nothing less. Cinderella has a stepmother and two stepsisters, but we know very little else about any of these characters.

In contrast, Walsh says, modern stories present characters in a reasoned narration, and not just as filling familial roles, "but as free autonomous spirits, whose destiny is personal fulfillment." Each characters is "... a unique individual with a unique personality, quirks and characteristic strengths and weaknesses, and a lively inner world of his or her own" (pp. 26-27).

In a current picture book version of Cinderella, the young woman must be reborn as a strong individual personality, a unique character. For an example, watch the movie *Ever After*. Here, the Cinderella character loves the land, has a passion for life and learning that surprises and delights the Prince. She doesn't need a rescuer because she's a strong enough character to stand up to the villain herself; in fact, she rescues the Prince from the Gypsies with her wit.

CHARACTER ARC

Walsh's ideas have immense implications for writing picture books. I've written stories in which the role of the character is important, not the individual personality of the character: These stories don't sell. Modern stories celebrate the individual as unique, with well-rounded characterization. Listen to these comments from my rejection letters:

Dutton: "I'm afraid I can't offer it a place on our list because we aren't having much luck with folk tales in the current market."

Harcourt: "It's hard to distinguish the voice of each character; they both sound rather generic. . . . I find the narrative voice rather distancing; I don't respond to the girl as a character."

Scholastic: "I didn't feel that the narrators developed enough depth and personality to make the ending truly resonate for me."

When I first wrote a manuscript called "Paul Allen," everything in it was in the folk tale mode. Characters related to their environment and to each other in terms of roles: a small boy finds imaginative ways to fill his days. Beyond his imaginative skills, I did no character development, wrongly believing it not necessary in a picture book.

After thinking about the difference in folk tale mode and modern mode characters, I rewrote it as *19 Girls and Me* (Philomel, 2006). It's a picture book about friendship in a kindergarten classroom with nineteen girls and one lone boy. John Hercules Po (new name because he's now an individual!) is a character with a unique problem that he solves in unique ways. His big brother teases him that those girls will turn him into a sissy. Over the course of the picture book, John Hercules worries about this, and the reader understands more of his inner life. In the end, he rejects his brother's ideas and proclaims that he has "nineteen friends." He now has a character arc appropriate for a picture book.

BEYOND PREMISE

About plots for picture books, Walsh says folk tales must be understood as symbolic, not rational. She cites the story of Oedipus, who kills his father and marries his mother: "If ever a story was symbolic, this is it; but in the moral universe of the modern world it does not make sense."

In Cinderella, Walsh points out all the illogic, the incoherency: sitting in ashes, a father who does nothing to help a beloved daughter, dancing in a glass slipper that is the only piece of finery to remain after midnight, a prince who can't remember the face of the girl he danced with the night before.

Rational dissection, Walsh says, doesn't work for a folk tale.

When I read that, I wanted to cheer! This is exactly how I've felt when editors read and commented on my picture book manuscripts:

Greenwillow: "Parts of the story are hard to believe."

Harcourt: "Many of the reasons behind plot events or characters' actions are rather unbelievable or seem undeveloped."

Dial: "I'm afraid the plot had substantial logic problems. "

Candlewick: "I'm sorry not to have been more convinced by the story."

If my picture book manuscripts were considered as folk tales—if my characters are fulfilling designated family roles and the stories are symbolic—then the logic or lack of it shouldn't be a problem. But in reality, editors consider stories as rational, believable, developed, convincing. Sadly, none of my folk tale approaches to a picture book story have sold. Walsh's article helped me to understand why: I need a new paradigm for picture book characters.

In some ways, I'm rephrasing an old problem. A story premise and a plot are two different things. The premise is the idea that sparks a story, and the plot is what actually happens. But it goes deeper, to the heart of character. Cinderella has a plot with a strong beginning, middle and end. But she's never pulled out of that folk tale role. Today's stories demand a character who is an individual, not a stand-in for a certain role. In *19 Girls and Me*, I changed a "creative kid" role into a boy stuck in kindergarten without any other boys for a friend. His creativity–instead of being the point of the story–became a character quality that propels him toward a resolution of his problem.

What I had been looking for in my picture books was a fairy godmother who could make my stories shine like a glass slipper. But maybe I don't need her help any longer. With my new paradigm for picture books, I just need to sit down with my characters and have a nice long chat about what's really going on with them.

ACTION POINTS

Find picture books that retell a folk or fairy tale and decide what approach the author took toward characters. Are the characters filling a particular role, or do they come alive as individuals? If a character fills a static role, how could you give the character "a free autonomous spirit"?

GENRES

In this section we'll discuss writing picture books in different genres. The ABC genre only exists for picture books. Because of the audience's age, some genres present challenges in simplifying the plot or vocabulary. Poetry is especially tricky because, while everyone loves Dr. Seuss, great poetry is very hard to write. And of course, the picture book format also accommodates a variety of non-fiction topics. Here's what we'll cover:

How to Write an ABC Book
How to Write a Great Read-Aloud Book
How to Write a Rhyming Picture Book
Bibliography of Rhyming Picture Books
How to Write a Poetry Collection Picture Book
How to Write a Picture Book Mystery
How to Write a Humorous Picture Book
How to Write a Picture Book Biography
How to Write a Creative Non-Fiction Picture Book
How to Write a Meta-Fiction Picture Book

HOW TO WRITE AN ABC BOOK

Within the picture book genre, one of the most popular sub-genres is the ABC picture book.

STORY ORIENTED ALPHABET PICTURE BOOKS

If you want to write an ABC book, you should first read *Chicka Chicka Boom Boom*, a rollicking story with the alphabet chasing around and having fun. It's a great example of what you can do with those staid letters if you want. But also be aware that this classic is your competition! A 2016 ABC title with a strong story is *Oops, Pounce, Quick, Run!: An Alphabet Caper*, which features a dog and mouse in an epic chase.

TOPICAL ALPHABET PICTURE BOOKS

But usually, people think of an ABC book about a certain topic like Dori Butler's *F is for Firefighting* book. This type ABC book uses the alphabet as a way to discuss different aspects of a topic, or as a way to organize a non-fiction topic. Remember that your audience is pre-school up to maybe second grade, or ages 3-7. Look for topics that will interest them, ones that can be used in classrooms.

To write a topical book like this, you should first apply the QXZ test. Usually, Q, X and Z are difficult letters to fill for your topic. No fair sticking X in the middle of a word: eXciting. No fair using Queen for every single topic. The words should be natural, not forced, and should be totally on-topic.

Actually, it's not just the QXZ test. For any given topic, those may be the easy letters, but there will be some letter that is difficult to find an appropriate key word. Before you get into the exact wording too far, think of the key words for each letter. If you do find a topic and have great keywords for each letter, then it's time to play around with the language. Again – look at *Chicka Chicka Boom Boom* for an example of just how far you can push it.

ALPHABET PICTURE BOOK MARKET

ABC books are hard. The market is glutted with them, and in order to stand out in "today's crowded market," your manuscript must really shine. It's a bit easier for illustrators who use the ABCs as a vehicle for their artwork. But for everyone, the competition is stiff — but not impossible. Most publishers will have one or two ABC picture books a year.

ACTION POINTS

Read a selection of ABC picture books, both topical and story versions.

Locate information on several publishers who might publish an ABC picture book.

Decide on a topic for an ABC book and try out the QXZ test. Are those the difficult letters for your topic, or did another letter cause problems?

HOW TO WRITE A READ ALOUD FRIENDLY BOOK

When revising a picture book, you must keep in mind that it needs to be easy to read aloud. Usually picture books are read to kids by adults. If you have to read the same thing over and over and over — and over again, then you learn to appreciate a smoothly written and fun text.

Read the picture book aloud. It seems obvious, but the first step is to read the text aloud. Over and over. When you're reading, make sure you never stumble on a phrase, never have to second guess where to take a breath. Revise until it is smooth and fluid. Rhythm is important here, not necessarily poetry, but just a lively sense of rhythm. If your writing seems boring, check your sentence lengths to make sure there is lots of variety.

Plan for an interactive story. Use a refrain or chorus that kids can quickly learn and chime in on when you get to that part. For example, in my book, *19 Girls and Me*, kids learn to finish the line, "Until. . . 'Lunch,' called Mrs. Ray." I think it's part of what put the picture book on the K-1 Read Aloud America list of recommended books (http://www.readaloudamerica.org/ books_K1.htm). Study books from their list, which is broken down by age levels, as examples of what to do right.

STUDY AWARD WINNING BOOKS

Besides the list above, also study winners of the E.B. White Read Aloud award, given by the Association of Booksellers for Children. One of my favorites is the 2004 winner, *Skippy Jon Jones* by Judith Bryon Schachner. It has great audience participation, great rhythm and is lots of fun. And the success of that first book has created a cottage industry with many new stories, books and products.

Put yourself in the adult reader's shoes. Think hard about the adult who will have to read this picture book multiple times. Is the topic one that can bear repeating? Is the language fun? Do the words roll off the tongue? Does the book foster the adult/child relationship? Taking the time to build in that read-aloud factor is the difference between a picture book that sells and drops within two years and one that becomes a real classic.

ACTION POINTS

Read a selection of picture books and try to decide if they are read-aloud friendly. What could you change to make them more read-aloud friendly?

HOW TO WRITE A RHYMING PICTURE BOOK

Often when people consider writing a children's book, their thoughts turn to poetry. Maybe it's Dr. Seuss's fault, or maybe it's a child's real love of rhythm and rhyme. Whatever the cause, it's true that most efforts at rhymed, metered poetry are so unsuccessful that editors say, "Don't send me any rhymed verse." Yet, many children's books are in verse. The key is that it must be pristine rhyme and meter, and right for this story. Here are some ideas that will help as you write a rhyming picture book.

First, everything you learned in school about poetry is incomplete. Traditional English poems do use accentual-syllabic poetry, but there are other options. If we include pre-Shakespeare, pre-Chaucer times, we find three types of poetry.

1) Syllabic poetry only counts syllables, such as Haiku.

2) Accentual poetry only counts the stressed syllables, and the number of unstressed syllables in between those stresses may vary.

3) Accentual-syllabic poetry counts all the syllables and the stresses.

Good Anglo-Saxon poetry was accentual because it focused on the number of stressed syllables; the French brought to England the practice of counting syllables, producing the accentual-syllabic poetry that is taught in schools today. A good example of accentual-syllabic poetry is the old standby, iambic pentameter. Here, we won't talk about syllabic poetry because it's not usually rhymed. Usually rhymed picture books are either accentual or accentual-syllabic poems.

What follows is a quick introduction to poetry ideas that relate specifically to picture books. It's not a full description of poetry, definitions of poetic forms, not details on how to generally write poetry. Consult a good poetry instruction book for details on general poetry.

ACCENTUAL POETRY

Accentual poetry is often the poetry form used in folk songs, ballads, nursery rhymes, and children's books.

Consider the opening of Sandra Boynton's board book for toddlers, *Moo, Baa, La, La, La.*

> "a COW says MOO./ a SHEEP says BAA./ THREE singing PIGS/ say, LA, LA, LA. "

It might appear to be iambic (da DUM) at first, but the third and four lines throw this off. In the third line, the stress comes in the first and last syllables (DUM da da DUM), and line four has three stresses and one unstressed syllables. (da DUM DUM DUM) Yet – read this aloud. It works! Why? Because the poem is mostly concerned with the accents. Lines two and four rhyme, giving us a rhyme scheme of xaxa or abcb.

Stepping up one level would be poems which are still accentual poetry, but now add consistent rhymes. The ballad or hymn stanza is a common example. Again, it could be described as having a four-line stanza with alternating iambic tetrameter and iambic trimeter and rhyming scheme of abab.

> From the familiar hymn, "Amazing Grace: "
> aMAZing GRACE, how SWEET the SOUND, a/8
> that SAVED a WRETCH like ME. b/6
> i ONCE was LOST, but NOW am FOUND, a/8
> was BLIND but NOW i SEE. b/6

True ballads, in fact, vary this strict form by adding an extra anapest (da da DUM) or two in each stanza; these extra syllables go back to the accentual form where the syllable count doesn't matter, only the accents. This small metrical difference can speed up the rhythm and thus a narrative. On the other hand, literary ballads are more likely to stick to the accentual-syllabic meter.

When you are writing children's picture books, no one will fuss at you or even care if you use accentual or accentual-syllabic poetry, as long as it works. And in fact, often the accentual poetry works better for some stories because it gives you more freedom in the text.

ACCEPTABLE VARIATIONS OF METER

The second thing not taught to high school students about poetry is that there are acceptable variations for almost every meter pattern. Longfellow is often accused of being too strict in his poetry, so strict that his poems might put a person to sleep! There's no need for that when there are acceptable variations for each rhythm.

Here are some substitutions of one foot in a line of iambic pentameter: the lines would still be considered acceptable lines in an iambic pentameter poem. Note that if you change more than one foot per line, the ear fails to hear the normal meter and the line falls apart.

Normal line: daDUM daDUM daDUM daDUM daDUM
Spondee in first foot: DUMDUM daDUM daDUM daDUM daDUM
Trochee in third foot: daDUM daDUM DUMda daDUM daDUM
Amphibrach in the fifth foot: daDUM daDUM daDUM daDUM daDUMda
Catalexis, or dropping the last syllable: daDUM daDUM daDUM daDUM da

(See Turco, Lewis. *The Book of Forms: A Handbook of Poetics*, Third Edition. Hanover: University Press of New England, 2000, p. 39-43.)

There are other acceptable variations, and I recommend Turco's book if this interests you. The point here, though, is that there are acceptable variations. So, why do so many people insist on a strict count? Usually, it's not because they object to one of these substitutions; rather, there's something off in the rhythm of the poem; in other words, the wrong words in the wrong order. Most editors have limited exposure to poetic principles. But they do listen to the sounds of the poetry, and it must be perfect.

RHYMING

The hardest part of writing rhymed picture book texts, ironically, isn't the rhyme but the rhythm or meter. After dealing with rhythm at length, the actual guidelines on rhyming are few and easily dealt with. There aren't strict rules, but preferences; break any rule if your story demands it.

If you rhyme, then use perfect rhymes, not slant rhyme or near rhyme.

Use simplified rhyme schemes, such as rhyming only alternating lines.

Emphasize nouns and verbs; try to rhyme on a noun or verb, rather than an adjective, adverb, or other minor words.

Try using internal rhyme, where a word in the middle of the line rhymes with the last word in the line.

Finally, if you write poetry for children, use every poetic technique that makes sense: assonance, repetition, refrains, imagery, and so on.

RESOURCES FOR WRITING CHILDREN'S RHYMING PICTURE BOOKS

If you really want to write poetry and a lot of it, I recommend you start with these resources:

Baer, William. *Writing Metrical Poetry*. Cincinatti, Ohio: Writer's Digest Books, 2006.

Chaconas, Dori. Icing the Cake. http://www.dorichaconas.com/Icing%20the%20Cake%20page.htm

Kinzie, Mary. *A Poet's Guide to Poetry*. Chicago: University of Chicago Press, 1999, p. 307

Good rhyming dictionaries are useful, or use rhymer.com

ACTION POINTS

Read children's books looking for poetry lines that break the rhythm pattern in interesting ways. How does the author include other poetic techniques in the story?

RHYMING PICTURE BOOK BIBLIOGRAPHY

If you've been around children's literature long, you know that editors often say they do not want rhymed poetry. But they really mean that they want poetry that is perfect. Study these examples of successful rhymed picture books.

RHYMING NONFICTION PICTURE BOOKS

Graham, Joan Bransfiled. *The Poem that Will Not End* (2014)
McReynolds, Linda. *Eight Days Gone* (2012)
Paul, Miranda. *Water is Water* (2015)
Salas, Laura Purdie. *A Rock Can Be* (2015), *Water Can Be* (2014), *Woodpecker Wham!* (2015)
Shannon, George. *Who Put the Cookies in the Cookie Jar?* (2013)
Simon, Seymour. *Colors in Nature* (2014)
Ward, Jennifer. *Mama Built a Little Nest* (2014)
Weatherford, Carole Boston. *Freedom in Congo Square* (2016)

RHYMING FICTION PICTURE BOOKS

Agee, Jon. *It's Only Stanley* (2015)
Ashman, Linda. *Rock-a-Bye Romp* (2016), *Rain!* (2013)
Degman, Lori. *Cock a Doodle Oops* (2014)
Esbaum, Jill. I Hatched! (2014)
Finke, Margot. *Dreamtime Man* (2014), *Prairie Dog Play Days* (2014)
Fredrickson, Lane. *Watch Your Tongue, Cecily Beasley* (2012), *Monster Trouble!* (2015)
Klostermann, Penny Parker. *There Was An Old Dragon Who Swallowed a Knight* (2015)

Miller, Pat Zietlow. *Sharing the Bread: An Old Fashioned Thanksgiving, Whereever you Go* (2015)

Paquette, Ammi-Joan. *Ghost in the House* (2015)

Pinder, Eric. *How to Share with a Bear* (2015)

Rinker, Sherri Duskey. *Steam Train, Dream Train* (2013)

Schwartz, Coren Rosen. *Hensel and Gretel: Ninja Chicks* (2016)

Sudipta Bardhan-Quallen anything of hers, especially *Orangutangled*

Underwood, Deborah. *Interstellar Cinderella* (2015), *Bad Bye, Good Bye* (2014)

Yolen, Jane and Heidi Stemple. *You Nest Here with Me* (2015)

PINTEREST BOARD TO KEEP UP WITH NEW TITLES

https://www.pinterest.com/darcypattison/rhyming-picture-books

HOW TO WRITE A POETRY COLLECTION PICTURE BOOK

Poetry collections make great children's picture books. The most common type of poetry collection seen in picture books is 15-30 poems on a single, specific topic. For example, *Barefoot: Poems for Naked Feet*, by Stefi Wiseburd, is about feet and has 26 poems.

Focusing on one topic slots the book into a category for use in the classroom, as well as focusing your poetry. For likely topics, look at schools' curriculum and find a niche to fill. March is Poetry Month, and these type books are widely sought after during that time, so perhaps something related to spring or topics taught in the spring would sell better.

Within a topic, you can mix and match poetry genres. Another strategy, though, is to feature all one genre poetry, but vary the topics. One of my favorite books is *Technically, It's Not My Fault* by John Grandits, a collection of concrete, or shaped poems, on a variety of topics. The key is to focus the collection of poetry, either on a topic or within a genre of poetry.

Another resource comes from Jack Prelutzsky, who was named the Children's Poet Laureate in 2006. His book, *Pizza, Pigs and Poetry: How to Write a Poem* is for kids, but you'll learn from it, too. Also read, *Button Up! Wrinkled Rhymes* by Alice Schertle, and watch her perform from it (http://youtu.be/Y-aYviJUtCs).

ACTION POINTS

Read several collections of poetry. Think about why the topic of the poems would appeal to kids and teachers. List five topics you might write about.

Locate information on several publishers who might publish picture book poetry collections.

HOW TO WRITE A PICTURE BOOK MYSTERY

Picture book mysteries are rarely for the pre-school set; instead, the audience is the early grades, K-3. For these kids, the core of the mystery needs to be something gentle, non-threatening. No murders here. But strange situations, natural disasters and chase scenes work well.

Puzzles or Strange Situations. *In The Mystery of Eatum Hall*, by John Kelly and Cathy Tincknell, Glenda and Horace Pork-Fowler, a goose and hog of "large proportions" are invited to a weekend of free gourmet food at Eatum Hall. In spite of great feasting, it's a strange place and an even stranger pie-eating festival is planned for the last day. Will they eat their way out of this Hall? Lots of visual puns and lots of fun.

Natural Disasters. Author/illustrator Ellen Stohl Walsh has a great series of picture book mysteries about two mice, *Dot and Jabber*, who must solve mysteries dealing with nature. In the *Mystery of the Missing Stream*, a storm knocks limbs and leaves into the stream, drying it up. Dot and Jabber must travel upstream to find and dislodge this dam. Though it's a gentle mystery, it still has the appeal of clues for kids to follow.

Chase Scene. In my book, *Searching for Oliver K. Woodman*, a wooden woman detective, Imogene Poplar, P.I. chases the wooden man, Oliver K. Woodman across the United States. Clues are provided in newspapers, by glimpses of the missing hero, and stories told in letters or postcards. It's essentially a chase scene, one of the major components in a mystery. Again, the clues are easy to follow but provide variety to keep a reader's interest.

Because they require more complicated thinking skills, mysteries really take off when kids reach the easy-reader level. But picture book mysteries are still successful in introducing the genre to kids.

ACTION POINTS

Read a selection of mystery picture books. What kind of mystery is presented? What age range is the book for?

Locate information on several publishers who might publish picture book mysteries.

HOW TO WRITE A HUMOROUS PICTURE BOOK

To understand what kids think is funny, you must read Paul E.McGhee, Ph.D, the guru of kids' humor. See his book, *Understanding and Promoting the Development of Children's Humor* at www.laughterremedy.com

Here's a summary of his stages of development of humor in kids.

0-6 months: Laughter without Humor
Few, if any picture books for this group include humor.

6-15 months: Laughter at Attachment Figure
You'd need personalized picture books to evoke humor here because you need the specific person. This is when the adult reading the book can add humor, though, by playing with the story and reading it with expression and by changing the text, tone of voice, etc.

2-4 years: Misnaming Objects or Actions
Kids deliberately misname an object or action to see what the adult says. For a great example of this, look at *Blue Hat, Green Hat* by Sandra Boynton. In this delightful book, the turkey consistently puts on the wrong item of clothing.

3-5 years: Playing with Word Sounds
Ever wonder why so many editors emphasize word play for kids? Here's why. Kids think it's funny. *The Recess Queen* by Alexis O'Neill is funny, partly because of the great language: "Kits and Kajammer 'em."

5-7 years: Pre-riddle Stage

Here, kids understand the form of a riddle, but don't understand vocabulary enough to understand what is funny and what isn't. This is the age of almost incoherent knock-knock jokes:

Knock-knock.

Who's there?

I like waffles! (Child giggles hysterically.)

6-8 years: Riddles

For this stage, all the joke books apply. Kids love to read, hear, and tell jokes of all kinds. They read *Amelia Bedelia* by Peggy Parish for its great plays on word meaning. True humor has started to emerge.

If you want to write a humorous picture book, make sure you are targeting a specific age group and understand what is funny to them.

ACTION POINTS

Read a selection of picture books, looking for humor. Do you think your sense of humor matches a child's sense of humor? Try to find something humorous for each age-level child.

HOW TO WRITE A PICTURE BOOK BIOGRAPHY

Picture book biographies are hot commodities these days, but they are very hard to get right. Remember that picture books are 32 pages and are usually written for kids below ten years old. The problem is how to cover the entire lifetime of a person in just 32 pages. Well, you can't. Besides that, kids less than ten years old have lived most of their lives in the Twenty-first Century and won't know that famous person you want to write about. Both topic and genre are against you.

Still, there are successful picture book biographies, and they usually focus on the narrative arc and/or the emotional core of the person.

NARRATIVE ARC

Wilma Unlimited: How Wilma Rudolph Became the World's Fastest Woman by Kathleen Krull is the picture book biography of how the Olympic champion overcame childhood illness and became a world class athlete. The narrative arc is strong: obstacle, obstacle, obstacle, success. It's a classic plot line of a character who wants something, but faces obstacles until there's a resolution.

When considering a person as the topic of a picture book, look at the person's life to find a narrative arc. Remember that picture books are a visual medium and think in terms of strong verbs and illustration possibilities.

EMOTIONAL CORE

If you can't find a narrative arc in the person's life, then look for the emotional core of the person. *Frida* by Jonah Winter is organized around the idea that this artist turned her pain into art. It's not so much the narrative arc that carries the biography as the build up of emotional impact on the reader.

Again, look for the core of the person, illustration possibilities and a way to build the emotions.

UNSATISFYING TO SOME NON-FICTION FANS

Many picture book biographies are unsatisfying to those who often write non-fiction. "Just the facts, ma'am" doesn't come through, especially for a biography that emphasizes the emotional core of the person. But really – how can you get a kid interested in someone who's been dead for a long time? Especially when you only have 32 pages. The audience for a picture book biography affects what you emphasize, even as you make sure you have the facts straight. Kids don't care what the person DID; instead, you must engage kids with the person's character and personality.

Jonah Winter's picture book biography of jazz musician Dizzy Gillespie, entitled *Dizzy*, is a good example of a story that is lighter on the facts than some might like; yet, it received six starred reviews and connects with kids in a special way.

WHO TO WRITE ABOUT

Another difficulty is finding the right person to write about. It should be someone famous for something. But if the person is too famous, there may be too many stories already about that person. If the person isn't famous enough, then it's hard to sell the book. Finding a person on the cusp of becoming famous is hard. Education presses are more likely to feature a person's biography if they can tie it to the curriculum in some way.

ACTION POINTS

Read a selection of picture book biographies. What approach is taken in your favorites? Locate information on several publishers who might publish a picture book biography.

Make a list of biographies you might want to write. Check to see if there are already books on the person. If you find several, it doesn't mean you can't write one, too. You must simply find a unique approach to the story.

HOW TO WRITE A CREATIVE NON-FICTION PICTURE BOOK

Non-fiction is about the facts. But those facts cannot be trite, boring, or presented in a cliched way. Instead, you must find creative ways to present the material to the kids. Here are some examples of how writers have solved the problem.

Poetry. *The Seldom Ever Shady Glades*, by Sue Van Wassenhove, evokes the Florida Everglades in poetry. Or, look at the *World Snacks* series by Amy Wilson Sanger, which began with *The First Book of Sushi*.

Creative Language. Language play doesn't have to be pure poetry, but can just evoke a poetic feel. Or it can evoke a certain place or time period. Or, use a concept that kids are just learning. Laura Vaccaro Seeger, in *First the Egg*, uses the pair of concepts, First -Then. Or, read my picture book, *Prairie Storms*, a lyrical text about storms on the prairies; it was written first as poetry, then changed to prose, keeping much of the poetic feel.

Illustrations. Of course, illustrations can add to the effectiveness of the use of facts in a picture book. Nic Bishop's amazing photography was the starting point for the non-fiction book, *Red-Eyed Tree Frog*, with text by Joy Cowley. Whether the illustrations/photography comes first or last, think about how to integrate the text and words.

HUMOROUS NONFICTION

A special category of creative nonfiction includes books which make you laugh. Study some of these books to see how they do it. Notice that some of these nonfiction titles are 40 or 48 pages, longer than the normal 32 pages.

This allows the author to include more facts. And often, there is creative layout and design to showcase facts in a humorous way.

Anderson, Laurie Halse. *Thank you, Sarah: The Woman Who Saved Thanksgiving*
Arnold, Tedd. *Manners Mash-Up: A Goofy Guide to Good Behavior*
Kerley, Barbara. *What To Do About Alice*
You Wouldn't Have Wanted To... series
Magic School Bus (faction)
Lauber, Patricia. *Fingers, Forks, & Chopsticks*
Hansen, Amy. *Bugs and Bugsicles: Insects in the Winter*
Pattison, Darcy. *Burn: Michael Faraday's Candle*
Stewart, Melissa. *It's Spit-acular: The Secrets of Saliva*
Goodman, Susan E. *The Truth About Poop, Whiz*
Krull, Kathleen. *Fartiste*
Walsh, Melanie. *Do Pigs Have Stripes?*

ACTION POINTS

Read a selection of nonfiction picture books. What topics are done well, and which seem weaker to you?

Locate information on several publishers who might publish nonfiction picture books.

HOW TO WRITE A METAFICTION PICTURE BOOK

A REVEALING CONVERSATION BETWEEN DH AND ME

Me: I need to write a blog post about metafiction picture books.

Darling Husband (DH): What's that?

Me: You know. Postmodern stuff.

DH: What?

Me: They are books that refer to themselves in some way. They break the concept of "book" in the story itself.

DH: Oh. Faux books.

Metafiction picture books are those that break the mold by making the reader aware that they are reading a book. Often fiction writers talk about the immersive book and value stories that transport a reader to a fictional world and which immerses them totally in the story. The reader's surroundings disappear, and they are deeply involved with the story.

Metafiction breaks that immersive experience. Why? In the theater, this is referred to as breaking the fourth wall. The stage has a back wall and two wings; the fourth wall is the invisible wall that separates the audience from the stage. When an actor turns to the audience and makes comments, s/he is breaking the fourth wall. The technique can be used to add information, set up irony, create humor or other purposes.

While metafiction isn't new, it's been more prevalent in the last few decades. Some say that it's related to the postmodern philosophy. Read more about postmodernism on Wikipedia.org (https://en.wikipedia.org/wiki/Postmodernism).

So, what is a metafiction picture book? Let's look at some characteristics typical of this genre. Of course, you won't use all of these in any given book. You can mix and match techniques to tell your story (or un-story). The best way to understand these is to read through a variety of the books suggested below.

CHARACTERISTICS OF A METAFICTION PICTURE BOOK

FURTHER CONVERSATION WITH DH

Me: One reason I need to write about metafiction is because I've been trying to critique some manuscripts, and I'm having a hard time.

DH: You expect them to be a certain way and they aren't.

Me: Well. Yes. There are rules about writing picture books.

DH: Are there?

Here are some common characteristics of a metafiction picture book:

Parody or irony. Some metafiction picture books refer to folk or fairy tales, often with irony or parody.

Who's Afraid of the Big Bad Book? By Lauren Child

Pastiche. Copying a certain style of art to create something very different, these are usually author-illustrator stories. *Willy the Dreamer* by Anthony Browne.

Story gaps. Sometimes the text has gaps that require readers to make decisions about the story and its meaning. Academics call this interdeterminancy. *The Three Little Pigs* by David Wiesner.

Multiple narrators or characters. The story includes multiple point-of-view characters, often with multiple story arcs. *In Chloe and the Lion* by Mac Barnett, illustrated by Adam Rex, the author, illustrator and main character each tell separate stories and talk to each other. The complex interaction has three separate endings.

Other books with multiple narrators:

Stinky Cheese Man and Other Fairly Stupid Tales by Jon Scieszka and Lane Smith

Black and White by David Macauley

Voices in the Park by Anthony Browne

Direct address to reader. When you use second person point-of-view and talk to the reader, the story can fall into the metafiction category. In a quick review of different points-of-view, you can usually figure out the story's POV by looking at the pronouns.

1st person: I, me, my
2nd person: You, yours

3rd person: he, she, it, his, hers

In *Warning! Do Not Open This Book*, by Adam Lehrhaupt, the reader is warned against opening the book. When—of course—the child does open the book, the text provides other warnings.

Other books with direct address to the reader: *Thank You, Sarah: The Woman Who Saved Thanksgiving*, by Laurie Halse Anderson,

Non-linear, non-sequential. Most narratives follow a certain time sequence. This happens first, and then that happens. There's a beginning, middle and end. However, metafiction picturebooks create stories without a clear reference to time order. In *Black and White* by David Macaulay, each page is divided into four sections which tell different stories, and it's up to the reader to connect them. Or not.

Narrator becomes a character. The author or narrator of the story steps into the story and participates. In *Chester*, by Melanie Watts, a simple story devolves into an argument between a cat and the author about what story to tell.

Unusual book design or layout. Some metaficiton picture books have unusual typography, while others use a layout that breaks the story out of the page or book. *Three Little Pigs* by David Wiesner has illustrations showing the pigs folding up a page and climbing out of the story onto a blank page. Or, they fold up a page into a paper airplane and take a ride.

Stories within stories. *No Bears* by Meg McKinlay, Ella writes a book within the book.

Characters who comment about their own or other stories. In *Chester* by Melanie Watt, the author and cat character go back and forth about the story. Among other shenanigans, the cat crosses out the author's name on the cover and puts his own name.

Disruption of time and space relationships. In *Redwoods* by Jason Chin, a boy picks up a nonfiction book about redwood forests and enters the forest.

Something makes the reader aware of what makes up a story. In *Help! We Need a Title!* By Herve Tullet, characters realize someone is watching them (that's YOU, the reader) and decide to make up a story. In the end, they invite the author to help finish the story.

Mixing of genres. In *A Book* by Mordecai Gerstein, a girl runs into characters from different genres in a search for her own story. This allows the reader to learn about elements of different genres.

Metafiction + Creative nonfiction. Can you write a metafiction nonfiction picture book? Yes. These stories often mix informational text with fiction. *No Monkeys, No Chocolate* by Melissa Stewart and Allen Young features a couple of worms who make funny comments while the narrator explains where chocolate comes from.

WRITING A METAFICTION PICTURE BOOK

A REVEALING CONVERSATION WITH DH

DH: Actually, I do metaficiton.

Me: What? When?

Flashback to memory of DH telling bedtime stories to our kids:

"Once upon a time, there were four bears. Flopsy, Mospy, Cottontail, and Peter Bear."

Me: (Slapping forehead) Oh, my goodness. You're a metafiction storyteller!

At least, there's one in the family.

Here are things to keep in mind as you write your metafiction story.

Know the Rules – Break the Rules. After reading this book, you'll know most of the "rules" of writing a picture book. For metafiction, break any rule that's reasonable for your story, but have a reason to break it. You may want to inject humor, parody, information, or yourself into the story for a good reason. Do it. And do it boldly.

Metafiction Topics. While you can write about anything, often the topic of a metafiction picture book is to explain a book or some element of fiction or writing. That's reflected in titles such as *It's a Book*, *There are No Cats in This Book*, and *Who's Afraid of the Big Bad Book?*. Of course, if you try this, remember that you'll have lots of competition.

Good Read Alouds. Make sure these are good read alouds because youngest readers may read these with adults to make sure it's understood. Review the section on writing a read-aloud book.

Have fun. One of the main reasons to write a metafiction picture book is to have fun, to play with the genre. Do something unexpected, disrespectful, funny.

A CONVERSATION ABOUT CRITIQUING METAFICTION PICTURE BOOKS

DH: Actually, I like a lot of the books you're calling metafiction.

Me: Why?

DH: They're unexpected. A surprise. They make me laugh. Kids love them.

An aside: In my household, it's understood that I don't have a sense of humor.

Slap stick? No, it's not funny.

Potty jokes? Absolutely not.

Metafiction? I'm not laughing.

DH: Of course it's hard for you to critique metafiction manuscripts.

Me: (Groan. Why is he always right?)

DH: (Wisely, DH refrains from saying anything else.)

Authors, give your group (or editor) a heads up. When I approach a critique of a picture book, I am always expecting a traditional story. So, it's helpful if the author is aware of the type picture book they are writing and can tell the critique group, "This is a metafiction picture book."

Readers, read the story in front of you. I often read movie or book reviews and get aggravated because the review is more about the reader than the text. The reviewer talks about what they wanted or predicted and how those preconceptions were disappointed. That's the danger in critiquing this special type of picture book. Especially for metafiction picture books, you must read the text in front of you. Be open to a new way of telling a story for kids.

RESOURCES: READ MORE

Hollingsworth, Ann Staman. Teaching Tip: Fun with Metafiction. July 30, 2015. Many Roads to Reading blog. Nice list of books and teaching tips. http://www.manyroadstoreading.com/teaching-tip-fun-metafiction/

Tantari, Sue. The Postmodern Picture Book and Its Impact on Classroom Literacy. C. 2014 http://tantaripostmodern.weebly.com/

Great explanation of metafiction picture books, including interactive elements, illustrations from selected books, charts and audio. If you're totally new to this genre, start here.

METAFICTION PICTURE BOOKS TO STUDY

Look for other titles by these authors, too.

Ahlberg, Allen. *The Pencil*

Barnett, Mac. *Chloe and the Lion*

Bingham, Kelly. *Z is for Moose*

Boynton, Sandra. *Moo, Baa, La, La, La*

Browne, Anthony. *Willy the Dreamer*

Child, Lauren. *Who's Afraid of the Big Bad Book?*

Chin, Jason. *Redwoods*

Freedman, Deborah. *Scribble*

Gerstein, Mordecai. *A Book*

Gravett, Emily. *Wolves*

Hopkinson, Deborah. *Abe Lincoln Crosses a Creek*

Lehman, Barbara. *The Red Book*

Macauley, David. *Black and White*

Schwarz, Viviane. *There are No Cats in this Book*

Scieszka, Jon and Lane Smith. *Stinky Cheese Man and Other Fairly Stupid Tales*

Smith, Lane. *It's a Book*

Spiegelman, Art. *Open Me. . .I'm a Dog!*

Stewart, Melissa. *No Monkeys, No Chocolate*

Tullet, Herve. *Help! We Need a Title!*

Watt, Mélanie. *Chester*

Willems, Mo. *We Are in a Book*

ACTION POINTS

First take time to read and reflect about some of the books listed above. Do you like this type of fiction? Or, like me, do you find it a challenging genre to enjoy?

If you like it, try your hand at writing a manuscript to see if you can work in the right touch of humor, irony and fun. Research publishers who might be likely to publish a metafiction picture book.

WRITE

It's time to write a story! Writing great stories for kids requires a general knowledge of what makes for good writing, a strong sense of story, and great use of language. Here are the topics we will discuss:

Good Writing: The Basics
Plotting the Picture Book
Plan Your First Draft
17 Picture Book Topics to Avoid
10 Suggestions for Picture Book Titles
Write
Did you Write a Picture Book or Something Else?
Let's Make a Dummy
From Shakespeare: 2 Ways to Look at Story Structure
Revise: Does It Hang Together?
5 Ways to Make the Reader Turn the Page
Phonics for Picture Book Writers
Create a Compelling Voice
Page 32
Picture Book Manuscript Checklist

GOOD WRITING: THE BASICS

This is a very brief review of elements of good writing. This book is focused on the picture book and includes only this short review on good writing in general. If you haven't written anything before, you may need to review some of the supplemental material suggested below.

USE SPECIFIC DETAILS

Good writing includes specific details: proper names, specific nouns, interesting verbs or exact descriptions. In the following examples, the second sentence uses more specific information.

Not this: The wind made noise and there was a noise like someone was following me.
This: Above the rustling wind came a soft scraping, a softer padding of feet on the bare rock path.

Not this: The big bird folded its wings, then dove at me.
This: Wings, golden honey on top, mahogany on the underside, stretched nearly twenty feet from wing tip to wing tip until the eagle folded them and plummeted.

Not this: The car went fast.
This: The car raced 356 miles an hour, a world record.

USE ACTION VERBS

Whenever possible, avoid the "to be" verbs (am, is, are, was, were, be, being, been, do, does, did, has, have, had, can, may, might, must, will, shall, would, should, could). Instead, substitute an active verb. In these examples, the second sentence uses stronger verbs and specific nouns.

Not this: The sun was shining.
This: Sunlight sparkled off the waves.

Not this: The boy is jumping up and down.
This: Michael bounced on the trampoline.

REPLACE WEAK MODIFIERS WITH STRONGER NOUNS OR VERBS

Use the most specific noun or verb first; only then can you add a modifier. In these examples, a strong verb or noun replaces a weak modifier. Modifiers are added, but only because the noun and verb are already specific.

Not this: The man walked slowly.
This: The man limped, favoring his injured right foot.

Not this: The dog was cute.
This: The frisky poodle made her laugh.

USE SENSORY DETAILS

Use a variety of sensory details. Most people include only visual details, or perhaps an auditory detail now and then. Instead, good writing includes all the senses: see, hear, taste, smell, touch (temperature/texture). In these examples, the second sentence has strong sensory details.

Not this: The stew was good.
This: Fragrant steam from the thick vegetable stew warmed his face. (specifics, smell, temperature/feel)

Not this: The dog barked.
This: The hound's deep baying sent chill bumps up my arm. (specific noun, feel, hear)

BE REASONABLE

Of course, be reasonable. Sometimes, especially for picture books, the best word is a more generic one. Use your judgment, but in general, err on the side of specific. Here is an example when the second sentence might be too specific.

72

Not this: Baby went to sleep.

This: Maria fussed and tossed before finally closing her eyes and drifting off to sleep.

USE DIALOGUE

For children's books, it is usually best to use a simple "s/he said," rather than any other speech tags.

Not this: "Time for bed," Mom coaxed.

This: "Time for bed," Mom said.

RESOURCES ON WRITING SKILLS

This is only a brief look at good writing skills. To brush up, I recommend this book: Brown, Dave and Renni King. *Self-Editing for Fiction Writers*, New York: HarperPerennial, 1993.

It's a basic look at editing your own work to make sure you Show-Don't-Tell, punctuate dialogue correctly, stay in the correct point of view, and much more. Easy exercises demonstrate the concepts of each chapter.

EXAMPLE OF UGLY WRITING

Sometimes, it helps to see bad writing in order to understand what is good writing. Here's a look at Ugly and Prettier.

UGLY

This is an example of a badly done draft of a picture book's opening:

Once there was a little boy who wanted to be a cowboy. He put on all his cowboy clothes. Then, he walked down to the corral.

The other cowboys were loading a big cow onto a truck. The biggest cowboy was amazing. The little boy wanted to be just like him.

"Can I help?" chimed in the little boy.

The great big cowboy laughed. "You think you can help at the rodeo?"

The other cowboys laughed, too.

The great big cowboy teased the little boy and finally the cowboys got in the truck and left him all alone.

PRETTIER

The following rewrite uses specific details and uses vocabulary, language and voice to evoke the setting. It's probably too long, but at least the writing is stronger.

Littlest Cowboy slapped on his one-gallon hat, his chaps, his spurs, and his boots.

He swaggered down to the corral.

Lester and the cowhands were loading Big Ben into the truck. Lester was a barrel-chested, bow-legged champion bull-rider, a real rodeo star, just like Littlest Cowboy wanted to be.

"I'm ready to go," Littlest Cowboy said.

Lester laughed. "Where are you going?"

"To the rodeo."

The cowhands leaned over the fence to watch the fun.

Lester said, "Well, pardner, there's just one problem. You're a mite too small to ride Big Ben. He's the meanest, oneriest longhorn in the Wild West. Why, you wouldn't even last one second on his back."

The cowhands sniggered.

One called, "He could run the barrel races with the girls."

The cowhands guffawed.

"But you said that if I cleaned out the horses' stalls, and cleaned the saddles, and learned to cook flapjacks, that you would teach me how to work at a rodeo."

Lester roared with laughter. "Why, pard', I though you knew. You're too little to ever do anything at a rodeo."

With that, the cowhands piled into the truck with Lester, and they drove away in a cloud of dust.

Note that the second version is longer. For the limited space of a picture book, it might need to be cut. As you consider cuts, make choices based on where you want the reader to pay attention.

GOOD WRITING IN A PICTURE BOOK

All the tips for great writing above apply to picture books. However, there are some additional hints about what makes for good picture book texts.

BE CONCRETE

Fear, thinking, dreading, imagining, wishing—these are all too abstract for a picture book. Think about how to make these concrete. Notice that as you do this, you'll be concentrating on strong nouns and verbs and sensory details.

Not: Brat the Cat was scared of mice.
Instead: Brat the Cat's paw quivered in fear when he passed by the mouse hole. At night, he avoided the mouse hole by going through the dining room.

USE DIALOGUE

Good dialogue can characterize and add interest and rhythm to a story. Be sure to keep the dialogue lively and cut out extraneous words. Dialogue can lengthen the time/space it takes to tell the story, so you need to balance length against the need for dialogue.

Not: Brat Cat didn't like his birthday presents because it was all about mice. Samantha and Julie gave him a toy mouse that made noises. He hated it.

Not: (Stronger details; but the dialogue is too long and wanders around.)
Brat cat opened his present from Samantha and Julie. It was a mouse toy.
Samantha punched it. "Do you like it? We got it yesterday and I really like how it sounds crackly."

Julie twisted its tail. "I helped pick it out, and it does sound crackly. But if you squeeze it just so, it makes a great squeaky noise, too."

But Brat Cat was a bad cat. He just backed away and wanted to stick his paws in his ears to stop the noise.

Instead:

Brat Cat opened his present from Samantha and Julie. It was a mouse toy.

Samantha punched it. "Do you hear that crackle?"

Julie twisted its tail. "Do you hear that squeak?"

But Brat Cat was a bad cat. He backed away and stuck his paws in his ears to stop the noise.

SENSORY DETAILS

Omit most visual details—only use the unique or mandatory ones. Use strong verbs for most kinesthetic details (how it feels to move in space). Use sounds whenever possible. Think of onomatopoeia possibilities. Use smells whenever possible. Use taste whenever possible.

ACTION POINTS

Read a selection of picture books and pay attention to the word choices, the writing itself.

PLOTTING A PICTURE BOOK

Like folk tales, picture books often have a tight structure. Here are some traditional plot structures that might work for your picture book.

Cumulative Sequence
This is the House that Jack Built is a good example of a cumulative structure. It begins with a statement, which is repeated with an addition, the two statements are repeated with the addition of a third; and so on.

Cumulative–Winding
An event is added with each repetition.
Example: *Bringing the Rain to Kapiti Plain* by Verna Aardema.

Cumulative–Winding, Unwinding
When all additions are made, the sequence is repeated, but this time, one statement is removed with each repetition, until the story is left with only the opening statement.

Number Sequences
The number of repetitions can be culturally based: 3, 4, 7, 9, 10, 12. Three repetitions (Three Little Pigs) is a northern European story, where three is an important number. In the Navajo culture, four is important: four cardinal directions; four sides of a hogan, etc.
Example: *Hush!* by Minfong Ho (10 repetitions)
Counting books can count by 1s up to 3, 5, 10, 20, or 100. Counting by 2s, 5s or 10s sometimes occurs in stories for older children.

Alphabet Sequences
A common way to organize a story is to choose words to match the alphabet sequence. See How to Write an ABC book earlier in this book.

Event-Repeat Sequence

An event repeats a certain number of times; sometimes the event repeats exactly, but sometimes there is a substitution. For example, in the Three Little Pigs story, the first pig receives straw, the second pig receives sticks, and the third pig receives bricks. The substitutions can occur in any position.

No substitution Example: *Gunniwolf* by Wilhemina Harper

Substitution Example: *Hush!* By Minfong Ho

Chronological Sequence

Chronological order is popular because kids are just learning about time. You can feature hours in a day, days of the week, months of the year, or seasons. Or, it might be the stages of something, like the stages of a journey.

Example of one day: *The Day of Ahmed's Secret* by Florence Parry Heide and Judith Heide Gilliland or *Desert Baths* by Darcy Pattison

Example of months of the year: *Prairie Storms* by Darcy Pattison

Journey Example: *The Journey of Oliver K. Woodman* and *Searching for Oliver K. Woodman* by Darcy Pattison

Cause-Effect or Action-Reaction

This is the traditional story where some event causes another event—it's a story with a traditional plot.

Example: *Fritz and the Beautiful Horses* by Jan Brett

Embedded Stories or Frame Stories

Sometimes, there is a frame story that begins and ends the book; however, in the middle is a separate story. Often the frame story is present day, while the inside story is a memory. This is a more complicated structure, not usually suitable for the preschool audience.

Example: *Knots on a Counting Rope* by Bill Martin, Jr., and John Archambault

Definition

Sometimes, a picture book might be an extended definition.

Q and A

The question and answer format can work for some stories. For example: a close-up illustration is accompanied by a jingle about an animal that ends, *"What am I?"*; when the page is turned, the reader sees the entire animal.

ENDINGS

When plotting a children's picture book, you should give special attention to the beginning and ending of the story. For more, see the "Page 32" chapter later in this book. For now, think about what type of ending will work best.

Circular endings. These stories come full circle and begin where they end.

Example: *How to Make an Apple Pie and See the World* by Marjorie Price-man

Climactic endings. This is the traditional ending, where events are wrapped up in an emotional scene at the end. Example: *Fritz and the Beautiful Horses* by Jan Brett

HERO'S JOURNEY

When the story is a cause-effect type story, often the character goes through a typical series of events on his/her journey to becoming a hero/ine. This type structure is more complicated than most picture books, but for a longer story, it can be used or adapted to the genre. Any event listed can be omitted, or one can be extended to fill a larger portion of the story. Here are the typical stages of the hero's journey.

Ordinary World or Opening Image: What is the ordinary world like for the character? The theme may be stated or be implicit in opening image.

Call to Adventure or Catalyst: Something happens to change the ordinary world. "One day, _____."

Refusal of Call or Debate: Often the character will resist the change.

Mentor: Sometimes, a mentor gives advice. This could be from a family member, a friend, an authority figure, a fairy godmother, etc.

1st Threshold or Breaking into Act Two: The events have forced the character to deal with change and conflict.

Tests, Allies & Enemies or Fun and Games: The character deals with challenges or has fun with the situation. Depending on the story, this can be language play, or it could make the situation much worse.

Bad Guys Close In: The events are worse, forcing the character into more conflict.

All is Lost and Dark Night of the Soul: The character must make a choice, often a moral choice or an unwanted choice, but one that will bring growth. Often, this is the place where the characters face the worst thing possible, the thing they fear the most.

Reward: This is a moment of fun or happiness because the worst is over (or so the character thinks).

The Road Back or Catalyst for Act 3: Here, the character must go home, or must face the change that has happened. Some event forces the character to go back toward the ordinary world, but things have changed, so the character faces that world in a different way.

Finale: There is a final resolution of the conflict.

Final Image: A final, satisfying, emotional look at our character.

For more on the Hero's Journey, see: Vogler, Christopher. *The Writer's Journey*. Studio City, CA: Michael Wiese Productions, 1992.

ACTION POINTS

Study several picture books and determine the structure. For example, if there are repetitions, count how many repeats occur. Look for several different kinds of plot structures.

17 PICTURE BOOK TOPICS TO AVOID

Before you start your story, let's talk about topics that have been over done in children's literature. For several months before Dial editor, Liz Waniewski (ONE–es-key) spoke at a conference, she kept track of her slush pile picture book submissions by category. At the conference, she presented the top 12 picture abook topics that she received–thus, the top 12 to avoid!

In this updated list, there are 17 topics to avoid.

It's not that these topics are taboo. Instead, they are so common that you must really rise above the competition to be accepted. For some topics, good examples of these topics are given, so you can study the competition.

Or as Waniewski put it, "Just because I see these topics many times doesn't mean you can't write about them. However, the competition is very stiff for picture books in these categories and your submission should really stand out in today's crowded marketplace." Knowing that many other writers are working on these topics should make us either avoid them entirely, or take our manuscript to that next level.

1) First Day at School. Good example: *19 Girls and Me* by Darcy Pattison.

2) Cleaning up your room. Good example: *Clean Your Room, Harvey Moon* by Pat Cummings.

3) Tooth fairy. Good example: *The Bear's Toothache* by David McPhail. A Little Brown editor once commented that this book has been in print continuously for 20 years and is still a steady seller for them. She said she'd love to see books that address kid-friendly topics in such a unique way. It's not

strictly a tooth fairy book because the fairy is just implied at the end. Still–it's a book about losing teeth, and the editor placed it in this category.

4) Christmas/Halloween

5) Wanting a pet. Good example: *I Want a Dog* or *I Want a Cat* by Darcy Pattison.

6) Dealing with a disability. These are too often message-driven; that is, the disability is the point of the story and it overwhelms the story.

7) "Hi! My name is_____and I am_____years old!" The hope here is that you establish a great character voice at the first. But this is too cliched.

8) Visiting Grandma and Grandpa.

9) We have a new baby.

10) Barnyard stories. Good example: *Farmer McPeeper and his Missing Milk Cows* by Katy Duffield.

11) Bedtime stories. Good example: *Rowdy: The Pirate Who Could Not Sleep* by Darcy Pattison.

12) Personal hygiene. Good example: *Everyone Poops (My Body Science Series)* by Taro Gomi.

13) Monsters acting un-monster-like.

14) Going Green.

15) "I Love You" stories. Good example: *You are My I Love You* by Mary-ann Cusimano.

16) Boredom. Good example: *I'm Bored* by Michael Ian Black.

17) Baby Bird Learning to Fly.

ACTION POINTS

Look for books that would compete with the topic you want to write about. Compare your idea with what's already out there: How does your book differ? What makes it unique? Why should someone choose your book over those on your competition list?

List picture book ideas but totally avoid these 17 topics.

PLAN YOUR FIRST DRAFT

It's time to write. The workbook section at the end of this book has several worksheets to help you plan your story. The worksheets are designed to make sure you think through the major elements of a story. You may not be able to fill in all the blanks at this early stage, but it will remind you of things to remember as you plan, write and revise. Choose the worksheets that help, and leave the others for revisions. Also, I'm presenting them in a chronological order, but you may want to work interactively across all the worksheets. Find the process that works for you.

Here are the main tasks as you write your picture book.

Plan your topic. Explore your topic and how you want to approach it.

Plan your characters. It's time to name your characters and delve into their background. Pay special attention to how each character changes over the course of the story.

Plan your setting. Even at this early stage, I like to plan the mood that the setting evokes. Choose sensory details that will evoke the mood you need for the story to succeed.

Plan your plot. Will you use a certain number of repetitions? Or an embedded story? Now's the time to play with options. Don't be afraid to try a couple before you settle on one.

Plot summary or synopsis. This exercise asks you to summarize your story in a single (very long) sentence.

Thumbnail sketches - optional. If you're more visually minded, you may want to plan the story by sketching. Think verbs and actions. What action possibilities have you given the illustrator on each page. Remember that the most deadly thing you could write would be Talking Heads, two characters dialoguing but with no actions to illustrate. Use the Thumbnail Layout work-page to draw sketches on each page to indicate what will happen. It doesn't matter if your drawing is chicken scratches, as long as it helps YOU visualize the structure of the story. Or if you prefer, jot down a verb on each page. The Thumbnail Layout will help you decide if there's too much or too little text to fit into the 32 pages. Adjust your story until the layout works.

Explore point-of-view options. Finally, you can explore the WAY you tell the story by looking at the point of view. I'd encourage you to try starting your story from each possible point-of-view. This has the most potential to impact your story in a good way.

ACTION POINTS

The Workbook includes seven planning tools. Take time to explore your story in multiple ways before you commit to just one structure. For some stories, one or another worksheet may be more helpful than the other, so you should be familiar with a range of options.

WRITE THE STORY

Using the ideas you've developed as a guide, write the story. Just write it. That's it. Write just like you would normally write any story. Keep in mind that you want it to be short and you'll leave visual details to the illustrator, but, otherwise, write the story.

DON'T WORRY

Picture book vocabulary doesn't have to be limited because usually an adult is reading the story to a child. Don't limit yourself on this first draft.

Don't worry about style. Just relax and write.

Don't worry about length. Remember you're writing a picture book, which implies you'll write short. But how short doesn't matter much on this first draft, unless you go over 10 typed double-spaced pages. Just write.

ACTION POINTS

Write.

10 SUGGESTIONS FOR TITLES

Once you have a draft, it's a good idea to make a stab at a title. This will likely change as you revise, and in the end, the publisher may prefer a different title. But this is a good place to start.

BRAINSTORMING TITLES

My best technique for finding a good title is to make lists. Long lists. Sometimes up to fifty or more titles, trying to find just the right phrase. Try some of these strategies as you brainstorm titles.

Use characters' names.
Include verbs or strong action words.
Use a metaphor.
Find a catchy phrase from the text.
Rhyme the title.
Play off a famous saying.
Include emotion.
Use something concrete.
Stick with the simple.
Be unexpected.

ACTION POINTS

Write 5-10 titles for your story. Choose the one you like best and use as a working title.

PICTURE BOOK OR MAGAZINE ARTICLE?

Have you written the first draft of your picture book? Good. Now, you need to check if the story is really a picture book text. Here's where the hard, yet fun, work begins!

Once I have a first draft in hand that I think might make a picture book, it's time to evaluate how well the story fits the structure of picture books and how illustratable the story is.

EDIT UNTIL THERE ARE 14-28 TEXT SEGMENTS

Begin by dividing your story into text segments, somewhere between 14-28; each segment represents what should go on a page or a double-spread page. 14 segments will give the illustrator enough text for double-page spreads for the standard 32 pages. 28 will give an illustration possibility for each single page. If you have somewhere in between 14 and 28 segments, it's fine because it means there is enough for the illustrator to work with, and you can safely leave the page divisions to the illustrator.

Please remember that the divisions and any story dummy you do are strictly for yourself to edit the story. When you send in the manuscript, do not include these page breaks; instead use a standard manuscript format.

As you divide the text into segments, you may discover that your story has too few or too many pages. Revise until you are at least close to the count needed. There is some flexibility in layout—the illustrator may include a word-less spread, or may decide to put two of your sections onto one page—but you must be close.

EVALUATE EACH TEXT SEGMENT

Once the page count is close, it's time to evaluate how well the story fits into the story book structure. Each text segment must do the following:

Advance the story. Something needs to happen! Action, reaction.

Provide an action for the illustrations. Overall, the story must move from setting to setting, so the illustrations can be varied. Of course, you can return to a setting, or the rhythm of the story may return to a setting several times. But each repetition must provide a new action or new details for the illustrator. The deadliest stories—and the least likely to be published—have talking heads. No action, just people talking. Inject some action into your story and choose the strongest verbs possible.

Make the reader want to turn the page. The reader should want to know what happens next. There are other ways to play with the page turns, but we'll get to that later.

Inevitably, there are weak pages that need work. Keep reworking the story until it meets the requirements of picture book structure and the need for illustration possibilities.

OR, DID YOU WRITE A MAGAZINE STORY?

What if the story just doesn't fit these requirements?

If there are too few illustration possibilities, you probably wrote a magazine short story for kids. Look for children's magazine markets that fit your story. You can also look at each requirement for special genres of picture books to see if your story fits one of them.

Can you turn a magazine story into a picture book? Sometimes. It usually means more complications for the character to overcome, or additional complexity without becoming too complex. Think about complications or difficulties the character might face, and think in terms of actions that can be illustrated. Keep rewriting until there are about 14-28 sections, as described above.

Did you write too long? You may be a novelist! If you feel cheated out of some of the scenes you wanted to include, consider whether the story might work as an easy reader or short chapter story.

ACTION POINTS

Evaluate your story. Did you write a picture book, a magazine piece, or the start to a novel? If it's not a picture book yet, brainstorm ideas to expand or cut until it does fit the picture book format.

MAKE A DUMMY OF YOUR PICTURE BOOK

When you're happy with the text of your picture book manuscript, it's time to make a mock-up, or what is usually called a dummy.

Picture books combine text and words in a short 32-page book. The structure is so unusual that you need a dummy to refine and polish your text. It can tell you which section of text is too long, give insight into the pacing of the story across the pages, help you spot needless repetitions and much more.

HOW TO MAKE A DUMMY

Take 16 sheets of typing paper and staple along one side. You may use either a portrait or a landscape orientation, your choice. Some like cutting the paper in half and using 8.5" x 6.5", in a landscape orientation. The late Sue Alexander recommended using brightly colored typing paper to simulate art and text better.

Number the pages in the bottom corners, if you wish. It will begin with a single right-hand page as page 1, and end with a single left-hand page as page 32.

Now, get out the scissors! Cut and tape your text into the dummy. Put the title on page 1, but leave pages 2-3 blank, as these are usually front matter, such as copyright page, half title page, or dedication. Now, you have a choice: you can start your text on page 4 for a double page spread, or just on the right-hand page 5. After that, the text should lay out across the full spread.

If you have an author's note or other back matter (glossary, sources, etc, such as for a non-fiction story), you'll need to reserve a couple pages for that at the end.

USE THE DUMMY TO REVISE

Here are some things you might notice:

The story doesn't fill up 32 pages, or there's too much text to fit. (Revise for length.)

Read the dummy aloud and listen to it. The story sounds awkward when read aloud. (Smooth out the language.)

Each page has enough text, but some spreads have a weak illustration possibility. (Strengthen your verbs.)

The story doesn't make the reader want to turn the page. (Add tension, or use one of the page turn ideas included later.)

If you skip reading a page, the story doesn't change. (Omit page, or add essential plot elements to that page.)

The story is unclear; no one can figure out what is happening. (Tighten the story; check transitions; write clearer.)

The story feels too wordy. (Cut in half!)

The pacing feels jerky. (Consider where you want the reader to speed up and where you want them to slow down. Revise accordingly.)

The story all takes place in one setting. (Consider moving the story around for better illustration possibilities.)

The story has too many settings. (Reuse some settings, but with a different perspective, different actions, etc.)

The story feels flat. (Work on the emotional impact of the story on the characters; work on language and voice.)

The story's narrative arc is weak. (Create more tension; put more at stake.)

Mocking up a picture book, making the dummy, can't be under-estimated for its help in pointing toward weak spots that need revision in a picture book text. Get out the paper, stapler, and scissors and mock up your book!

WHEN USING THE DUMMY, REMEMBER

The picture book dummy is just for you. This mock-up is just for you to use as you revise to make sure you fit the format. You would never send it in to the editor.

The published book may have different page divisions. The editor, art director and illustrator may decide that the story should be divided differently. That's fine. Your job is to give them enough illustration possibilities that they can visualize this as a complete book. If you've done that, then your job is done and their job of actually making a book begins.

ACTION POINTS

Make a dummy of your picture book manuscript and evaluate each section. Rewrite as needed.

Keep the Dummy Updated. As you go through the next few lessons and make changes to the text, cut and paste the current text into the dummy and go back through the questions again. Make sure all changes keep the story within the parameters of picture book structure.

HELP FROM SHAKESPEARE

When you're thinking about writing a picture book, the structure is important. With about 14 double-page spreads, it's time to turn to Shakespeare for some help.

SONNETS AND PICTURE BOOKS

I like to compare picture book structure to the structure of sonnets. A sonnet has 14 lines, while picture books can have 14 double-page spreads. So, taking a sonnet as an example of structure, you can imitate one of these sonnet structures.

1) The Italian Sonnet consists of an octave (eight lines) and a sestet (six lines)
Octave:
    Spreads 1-4 Set up character
    Spreads 5-8 Problem stated
Sestet:
    Spreads 9-11 Character tries to solve the problem.
    Spreads 12-14 The payoff

Or, think of it as the beginning, middle, end, payoff. Or problem, attempts to solve, failure and re-commitment to try, payoff.

Notice that in this structure, there is a pivot point—things change drastically—between spreads 8 and 9. There are two minor pivots, too, between 4-5 and 11-12. These are good places for a twist to turn the plot in a different direction.

2) The Shakespearean Sonnet: Three quatrains (four-line stanzas) and a couplet.

    Spreads 1-4 Problem stated

    Spreads 5-8 Attempts to solve problem

    Spreads 9-12 Problem solved

    Spreads 13-14 The payoff

The main pivot point here is between 12 and 13; minor pivot points occur between 4-5, 8-9.

Check the structure of your story and its pivot points to see if it is the strongest it can be.

ACTION POINTS

Consider if this structure would work for your picture book. If it's close, see if you can adjust the text and page breaks for this structure. If it doesn't work with this structure, it's not necessarily a problem. Just go on to the next lesson.

REVISING YOUR PICTURE BOOK TEXT

Overall, does the story hang together? In such a short story, you can't mention anything extraneous, at all. If you mention a cat in the first paragraph, the cat needs to be important. Look over the story and list all the elements. Have you used them to weave the story into a tight-knit whole? Edit out (cut!) the extras and use what's left for maximum effect in your picture book.

CHECK THE NARRATIVE ARC

The narrative arcs upward from the first mention of a problem to the climax scene. Even quiet picture books need some kind of arc. One easy way to do this in children's picture books is to use a progression of some kind (good, better, best; bad, worse, worst). Even stories with an event-repetition (think of the three little pigs) have a progression (hay, sticks, bricks--or inappropriate building materials to most appropriate). Make sure the story builds in some way, even if it's a gentle building to a gentle climax.

CUT THE STORY IN HALF

The hardest yet most beneficial task of editing is to cut out words. Try this: Cut the picture book text in half. Stop resisting! Do it!

Are you finished? No, you can't stop with only about a fourth of the story cut. Cut it in half.

When you edited out half the words, what's left? Is the story gutted? Or just the descriptions? Did you manage to salvage the story at all?

Along the way, you may discover some of these things:

You don't need a certain character, a scene, or piece of dialogue.

The story is stronger when it's shorter.

The story lacks the emotional punch when it's shorter.

Cutting totally changes the story (for better or worse).

Usually, cutting a story in half is cutting too much, something is lost: action, characterization, emotion, or language play. But usually, the story is stronger in many ways, too, because you were forced to evaluate every single word. Picture books allow for no fat!

The next draft of your picture book will probably be somewhere between your original draft and the half-length draft. Work with the text and story, trying to keep the writing as tight as possible, but still tell the story and tell it in the best way.

Work with the draft—editing, cutting and rearranging—until you are satisfied, then come back for the rest of this painful lesson.

MICRO-CUTS

Now, go back and edit out another 100 words. Again, it's an arbitrary number, but it works so well. Think of this as a poem, which is the tightest writing possible. Nothing extra, but nothing left out.

Examples of micro-cuts and micro-changes:

Instead of a prepositional phrase, use an adjective.

While you're at it, replace "to be" verbs with stronger verbs.

Unless it's part of the voice, cut out introductory words, such as well, in fact, first off and so on.

While you're at it, sharpen details.

While you're at it, replace "to be" verbs with stronger verbs. Yes! Check again!

Replace weak nouns with specific nouns.

While you're at it, replace "to be" verbs with stronger verbs. Yes! Again!

PASTICHE OR BORROWING FROM OTHERS - MENTOR TEXTS

Look around for picture books you admire. When you find one, rewrite your story in the same voice and style as the admired book. Do at least once, but repeat as many times as you can. Some people call this using a mentor text, which is a picture book that you admire for some reason and want to copy some element from it. Of course, you can't plagiarize, but you can open a story in a similar way. Perhaps the structure of the mentor text provides the right structure for your story. Make it a career-long habit to read other picture books and study why they work.

Some things you might learn:

Your voice is bland, or excitable, or unique.

The story changes when you change the voice or style.

98

The appropriate age of the reader changes as the voice or styles change.

Your default style has too much (adjectives, to be verbs, visual description, etc.)

ADD WORD PLAY

Read Alexis O'Neill's book, *The Recess Queen*, as a great example of playing with language. It turns a didactic story about bullies into a piece of literature that I'd read to anyone. In fact, when my college freshman students had to write an essay about bullies, I read it to them. Try to find places for language play in your story: repetition, onomatopoeia, rhymes, and so on.

ACTION POINTS

Revise! This is where the fun comes in, so revise and revise and revise.

5 WAYS TO MAKE THE READER TURN THE PAGE

One of the key things I check when revising a picture book manuscript is page turns. Have I given the reader any reason to keep turning pages, or does each page standalone and the reader doesn't care if s/he finishes the book?

CREATING PAGE TURNS

Here are some techniques to make the reader want to turn the page:

Questions. Ask a question or stop a sentence in the middle and carry it over to the next page. From *What Do You Do With a Tail Like This?*

What do you do with a tail like this? (Page turn.)
If you're a lizard, you break off your tail to get away.

Compound Words. Use only half of a compound word on one page and the rest on the next page. For a masterful use of this concept, look at Rick Walton's book, *Once There Was a Bull . . .(Frog)*.

Once there was a bull. . .(page turn) . . .frog who had lost his hop.

Transition words. Use key transition words. Then, When, But, And, Until. . .The ellipsis (punctuated with the three spaced-out periods) works here to let the reader lengthen the transition word, until the page is turned, revealing a new illustration, and the thought can continue.

Visuals. Strong page turns can be created with visuals – a tail (page turn) becomes the rest of the animal. Or, provide a close up on one page and on the next page, pull back to see the whole picture. There are lots of variations on using visuals to create an effective page turn. In general, the writer can't insist on the visual, but you can hint at it with your text.

Cause-effect. Of course, the final way to get readers to turn the page is to write an exciting story. If the plot is exciting, then readers will turn the page to find out what happens next.

ACTION POINTS

Evaluate your manuscript. Are there ways to make the reader anticipate the page turns? How can you add elements to maximize the page turns?

PHONICS FOR PICTURE BOOK WRITERS

Writing successfully is a combination of what is told (story) and how it's told. Here, we'll talk about the way the story sounds and how that affects the content.

Sounds are made by a combination of vocal cords vibrating or not vibrating, the shape of the tongue, lips, teeth, and the amount of tension put on each. Generally, we divide these sounds into vowels and consonants.

VOWELS

You remember this: vowels are are a,e,i,o,u. In phonics, though, each of these letters can have more than one sound. The variations of vowel sound formations in the mouth can be categorized on a continuum from high-front to low-back, referring mostly to the position of the tongue.

High Range–More Energy (tongue is high, front of mouth)

Long e	Tree
Short i	Sit
Long a	Play

Middle Range

Long i	Bright
Short e	Hen
Short a	Cat
Oi or oy	Toy
Ow	Chow

Low Range–Less Energy (tongue is low, back of mouth)

Ah	Far
Aw	Bought
Long o	Bone
Short oo	Book
Long oo	Boot

Dipthongs are vowels which combine more than one sound:
ow–combines short o with short oo–bow
oi–combines long o with long e–boy
Long u– y sound with long oo–s uit

CONSONANTS
Like vowels, consonants sound different depending on how the mouth is shaped.

Hard–b, d, k, p, q, t, hard c, hard g, z, ch, j
Soft–l, m, n, r, w
Sibilant–hissing sound–s, z, th, sh, zh, ch
Stopping sounds–b, p, m, n, d, t
Nasal–n, m, ng

Consonant Clusters combine several consonants and can have characteristics of several groups.

USING PHONICS IN A PICTURE BOOK
In my picture book, *19 Girls and Me* (Philomel, 2006), I paid attention to the vowels. If you say, "ah", you'll feel that the mouth is open, the tongue is down in back and everything is relaxed -it's a low vowel. If you say, "Eee", you'll feel your mouth tighten up and pull back, the tongue goes up in front and nothing is relaxed -it's a high vowel.

I decided to use the progression of vowels from low-relaxed to high-tense in the story, along with some assonance, or repetition of a vowel sound:

At noon on Monday, the kindergarten went out. (low vowels)

John Hercules saw a long ladder near the wall. "Let's climb Mt. Everest!" (Low to mid vowels)

Nineteen girls and one lone boy, they climbed and climbed. (Mixed to high)

They climbed so high, they reached the Yeti's peak. (High)

"Stay!" the Yeti cried. "Today, we play!" (Highest)

Nineteen girls and one lone boy heaved snowballs at the mighty beast until– (High)

104

What difference do these distinctions make? The high front vowels involve more tension in the mouth, while the low back are more relaxed. This mouth-tension can add to the felt tension of a piece of writing. By adding the vowel progressions, I added to the sense of going higher up a mountain.

WHAT'S THE POINT OF ALL OF THIS PHONICS STUFF?

The sound of your language makes more difference in picture books than anywhere else! Because the kids may not understand the connotations of the words, but they will hear the sounds, the rhythms, and the intonation patterns that comes from individual sounds. Controlling these means better control over the child's experience with your words.

For example, if you want to sing a lullaby, you'd try to keep as many of the vowels relaxed as possible. For action scenes, try for high front vowels.

Read aloud and listen to the sound of this stanza from *Rowdy: The Pirate Who Could Not Sleep*, by Darcy Pattison.

> Then Pappy sang of slumber sweet
> While stars leaned low and listened.
> And as the soft night gathered round,
> The pirates' eyes all glistened.

This stanza works in a bedtime story because of the repetition of s and l; also the use of low, relaxed vowels in slumber, stars, low, soft, round. The sounds of the story are relaxing and evoke the mood and feelings needed in a bedtime story.

These are common combinations of vowels and consonants:
Tense: High vowels, sibilant and hard consonants
Relaxed: Low vowels and soft consonants
Anxious: Nasal consonants and high vowels

ACTION POINTS

Revise your story, thinking about how it sounds. You may want to change names, find synonyms for objects or verbs, or add or subtract words.

CREATE A COMPELLING VOICE

The voice of a piece of writing is the overall effect of words, connotations, sentence structure, sentence length, phrasing, rhythm, the sound of the words and more. Voice is important, whether you're writing a novel or a children's picture book. One question that often arises is, "Can you revise for voice?" Yes. Here's an example of how it worked for me.

For example, in an early draft of picture book *19 Girls and Me*, I revised for an editor and sent him a version that started like this:

When John Hercules Po started kindergarten in Room 9B, it was an odd class. There were nineteen girls and one boy, John Hercules.

"You'll be a sissy," said John's big brother. He was in second grade and he was not a sissy.

"No, I won't," said John Hercules. "I'll turn those girls into tomboys."

On Monday, when the kindergarten went out for recess, a ladder was lying beside the wall. John Hercules called to the nineteen girls, "Let's climb that mountain."

Nineteen girls and one boy climbed Mount Everest and played with the Abominable Snowman until Mrs. Ray called them in to warm up with chicken noodle soup for lunch.

I thought I did a good job!

EDITOR'S REACTION TO FIRST DRAFT

The editor at wrote back:

"You clearly took my suggestion to heart, and have a stronger manuscript as a result. My sense is you're not all the way there yet, though. When I read this story, my gut is searching for a snap! of energy, to play alongside the soaring imagination of the children. Instead, the narrative voice feels bland, and so the energy level of the story remains somewhat grounded. You have a fun concept with true potential; now you just need to inject your narrative voice with some of that spirit in order to reach that potential. What I'd like to suggest is that you turn yourself loose (as you did when thinking of a new title); really inject some personality into the piece. It's always better to reign energy back in than it is to come up short."

SECOND REVISION

Oh, great! This editor is known for "buying voice" and he's saying, "the narrative voice feels bland." I was in big trouble! But, I had been studying voice, and I was ready to give it a try. A year earlier, I would have been in despair, not having a clue of where to begin. Now, I had some ways to start, things to look at, strategies to try. First, I thought that I would look at stress. In talking about words, I mentioned that the ends of sentences are positions of stress, especially if the word is a single syllable word ending in a hard consonant. In this sentence, what is the most important word? (Try to answer it before reading on!)

"When John Hercules Po started kindergarten in Room 9B, it was an odd class."

I thought that ODD was the most important word; it's also a single syllable word, ending in a hard consonant. I moved it to the end of the first sentence and started the revision of the picture book from there. Here's part of the revision:

The kindergarten class in 9B was odd.
"Nineteen girls," said John Hercules Po. "And me."
John's big brother shook his head. "What a shame! A sissy for a brother."
"Not me!" John Hercules said. "I'll turn those girls into tomboys."
At noon on Monday, the kindergarten went out. John Hercules saw a long ladder near the wall. "Let's climb Mt. Everest!"
Nineteen girls and one lone boy, they climbed and climbed. They climbed so high, they reached the Yeti's peak.
"Stay!" the Yeti cried. "Today, we play!"
Nineteen girls and one lone boy, they played beneath the Yeti's peak until–[Page Turn]
"Lunch," called Mrs. Ray.
Nineteen girls and one lone boy warmed their hands with soup du jour.

Same story, different voice; Philomel Books bought this version and published it as *19 Girls and Me*. And it sold Chinese, Arabic and German foreign language rights.

CHANGING THE VOICE OF YOUR STORY

We're into slightly fuzzy area in trying to revise for voice. I'll suggest some ideas here, but when you try them, you'll have to listen to the story. It takes some time to develop an ear for voice, but it's a worthy struggle.

Strategies to try:

Move single-syllable strong-ending words to the end of a sentence.

Vary sentence lengths. Count the number of words in each sentence and make sure you have lots of variety, from long to short. Don't be afraid of sentence fragments. Really.

As we learned in the last chapter, pay attention to the phonics, or how the words sound. Are they high or low vowels? Try using synonyms for some words to see if certain vowels work better in the story. In 19 Girls and Me, each day's activities started with low-vowel-words and progressed to high-vowel words. It worked because it echoed the increasing intensity of each day's play. Among other changes, I also changed the Abominable Snowman (low vowels) to the Yeti (high vowels).

Pay attention to the consonants. Consonance is often created by clustering consonants in any position in the word, from beginning to middle to end.

Cut out all adverbs. Cut out all adjectives. Or take the opposite approach and make the adverbs the point of the story. Or choose prepositions as the star of your show; i.e. objects are either over or under.

Cut the story in half. Double the story.

Find three different mentor texts, each with a unique voice. Rewrite three times, modeling a different story each time.

In the end, writers have limited tools: we only have words, sentences, phrases, and longer passages. To create a unique voice, you must create a unique combination of those elements. Experiment.

QUANTUM LEAP REVISIONS

I call this type of revision a Quantum Leap Revision because I'm not just looking at punctuation or grammar, but at the way I tell the story. This isn't a Pretend Revision, but a leap in how the story is told. Everything about *19 Girls and Me* was revised in the Quantum Leap Revision. You may change from poetry to prose or vice versa. Or you may change narrators. This type of huge story keeps something intact--character, events, theme--but everything else is up for major revisions. Once you know your story, then you want revisions that focus on HOW you tell the story.

Revising has two goals: what is the story I want to tell, and what is the best way to tell that story? Yes, they are intertwined and affect each other. But you can revise for voice. Consciously. Successfully.

Voice for children's picture books is part of what makes a good read-aloud story and part of what creates a unique picture book character. Experiment, read aloud, smooth out, cut, and revise in general with voice in mind.

ACTION POINTS

Take a good look at your story. Is the story working? Is it told in a compelling way? If you have any qualms at all, consider a Quantum Leap Revision.

PAGE 32: THE LAST PAGE OF A PICTURE BOOK

Page 32 is a left-hand single page. Consider ways to use this last chance to connect with the readers. It's the last chance to give the reader a twist, or emphasize an emotion. Here are some options:

Emphasize the emotional connection. In *Officer Buckle and Gloria*, by Peggy Rathman, the last page of this story about friendship between a safety officer and his police dog reads, "Safety Tip #101 'Always Stick with Your Buddy.'"

Begin the cycle again. *My Friend Rabbit* by Eric Rohmann is a story about friends who face a potential disaster together. On the last page, they start a new potential disaster.

Fulfillment. Sometimes a last page is simply the climax of the story, the fulfillment of the character's desire. In *When Marion Sang*, by Pam Munoz Ryan, the last page of the story reads, ". . .and Marian sang." In this story of opera singer Marian Anderson, she wasn't allowed to sing on many American stages because she was African American. In the end, though, "Marian sang."

Leave it to the Illustrator. Often the last page is a single-spread illustration with no words. It's a hug, a child sleeping, or the sun setting. These last images are a place for the adult and the child in the lap to have a moment of silence, or give each other that special hug. In *Nefertiti, the Spidernaut*, it's a last image of the Johnson jumping spider.

Nonfiction Last Pages. Nonfiction picture books tend to end with back matter: the author's note, the sources, maps, etc. In this case, refer to the last page of the text for the above. But also think about ways to cut down on back matter so the story carries itself. In *Dizzy*, by Jonah Winter, a story about the jazz musician, Dizzy Gillespie, (a book which received six starred reviews!), there's only one page of Author's Notes. It allows the reader to be fully in the story for almost the whole book. (Of course, sometimes a book needs more back matter, but cut when you can.)

ACTION POINTS
If needed, revise the last page of your story.

SUBMIT

Once you have written your manuscript, you need to submit it to publishers. Here, we'll discuss some of the ins and outs of the process. We'll look at these topics:

The Self-Publishing Option
The Biggest Mistake You Can Make in Submitting a Picture Book Manuscript
The Illustrator Doesn't Tell You What to Do
Titles and Subtitles Sell Your Work
How to Find an Editor's Name for Submission

THE SELF-PUBLISHING QUESTION

Let me say up front: self-publishing is a smart options for some books. To be successful, a self-published book needs some of these qualities, and the more the better:

1) A non-fiction topic dealt with in such a way that it meets the needs of the targeted reader.

2) A fictional story with superb writing, excellent copy-editing, good layout and design, and a good use of illustrations, along with a great marketing plan.

3) A narrowly defined niche market. For example, Wendy Kupfer's *Let's Hear it for Almigal*, a picture book illustrated by Tammie Lyon, celebrates Almigal's determination to hear every sound in the world with her new hot pink cochlear implants. It was named a Spark Award Honor book, the award given to self-published books by the Society of Children's Bookwriters and Illustrators (SCBWI).

4) A clearly-defined, easy-to-reach distribution channel. For example, I am a quilter, and the quilting industry in America is huge, with 27 million quilters and an industry that brings in $3.3 billion/year. It's a rather narrow market, though larger than many. The distribution channels are clearly defined: you go to Quilt Market in Houston every year (the spring market is still optional), and you'll get orders from every major quilt shop, quilt teacher, quilt catalog, etc. That's it. I know a quilting teacher who has a national reputation (she had built a platform -"the writer's reputation and public visibility – and the ability, willingness, and experience to promote themselves in the marketplace.") and decided to self-publish her next quilt pattern book herself. The first printing of 25,000 sold out in only six weeks. That's astounding!

Though not strictly necessary, if the author has a platform (see below) it helps.

SELF-PUBLISHING PICTURE BOOKS

Unfortunately, self publishing a children's picture book rarely has any of the elements listed above.

It is fiction, thus it doesn't meet any particular needs. It must live or die by it's literary appeal. Yes, I know that there are picture books about kidney transplants that help the child understand what's going on; I know there are picture books about how to deal with a chronically ill mother. But those are really non-fiction stories, wrapped with fiction.

Why do readers like fiction? Fiction exists to entertain, to inspire, to take your mind off something, to _____ (you fill in the blank). It's hard to pin down the appeal of a great book, and you can't target readers the same way you would in a non-fiction book. Which means, of course, that it's hard to market.

WRITING, EDITING, LAYOUT & DESIGN, AND ILLUSTRATIONS

Self-published books run the continuum from truly wonderful to truly awful. Unfortunately, the balance is tipped toward the truly awful side: too many people think their illustrations are worthy of publication; too many people skip the editing step in favor of having control over everything. This tipping of the scales toward the inferior end means self-published books, as a genre, have a terrible reputation. That has changed over the last ten years, but libraries, bookstores and many individuals still refuse to buy or stock self-published books becaue of quality-control issues. If you want to self-publish, you should hire a copy editor, book designer and a professional illustrator. But also think about your tolerance for criticism: can you accept criticism merely because you self-published, regardless of the quality of your book?

NICHE MARKET AND DISTRIBUTION CHANNEL

For children's picture books, the last two obstacles to self publishing are the niche market and the distribution channels. It's a narrow market, but you'll have immense difficulty getting distribution, which is "protected" by gatekeepers of children's literature such as children's librarians, school librarians and parents. You'll run an obstacle course to get into Scholastic Book Fairs, which sell directly to children through school programs. You'll be shunned by children's literature review journals. That means you must find catalogs targeted to parents or teachers, or buy mailing or email lists. Then your marketing model is one of direct-mail sales. (So, get thee to a library and read up on direct-mail marketing!)

The internet is supposed to be the great equalizer, but it only works if you can get the traffic to your site. Do you know how to set up a great website and then send 5000 people/month to see your offerings? And 5000 more the next month? Do you know how to convert traffic into sales?

How will you sell your book? How will you get the book into the hands of the people who should see it? That is the huge question that even traditional publishers ask themselves every single day.

On my blog IndieKidsBooks.com, I write about the issues of distribution, marketing, and sales. For a current discussion of the market, visit the blog.

THE ISSUE OF QUALITY, NOT CONTROL

Control. Some people get stuck on this issue. They want their book to say things a certain way, or to be illustrated a certain way. When an editor asks for changes, this type author disagrees with the suggestions and walks away. Personally, I think any editorial suggestions should be carefully considered and you should at least try it the editor's way. You can always go back to the first version. Often, failure to revise is the reason there are so many problems with the writing, editing, layout and design and illustration. The quality is poor, but the author fails to recognize this.

I know. You can go to the library or bookstore and point out any number of horrible books that got published anyway. I do the same thing. But someone had to believe in those books to make it to that point. Probably those books will not sell well and they won't stand the test of time. The point here is to compare your book to the best the market offers: those books are your true competition, not the awful books.

And, yes, there are times when your vision of the book isn't matched by the editor's vision, and you should walk away. In those cases, search for a more appropriate editor/publisher.

But at this point some writers are very frustrated and say, "I just want it out there." But merely "Out There" doesn't mean it will be in bookstores, or even find a place in the digital ebook market. Mostly likely, it will languish with less than 100 books sold. That's the typical fate of a self-published book.

To sell well, you must meet the high, yet fickle, standards of the marketplace. And you must back it up with a great marketing plan.

If you can sell the books, there's more profit. If you are a marketing guru, or have a huge fan base of 200,000 for something else you do, you will make more profit by self-publishing. Per book, your profit margins will be very nice and you won't have to sell as many books as a traditional publisher to make money.

MATH FOR SELF-PUBLISHERS

Let's say you publish Book A with a major publisher and the contract terms are for 5% royalties on list price, a typical offer on picture books because the illustrator also gets 5%. If the book lists for $10.00, the author receives $0.50 for each copy sold. To make $1000 on your share of the profits, your book must sell 2000 copies. However, if you self-publish Book B, you may have $4 profit from each copy sold because you don't have to share the profits (Unless you share with the illustrator.) Now, you only need to sell 250 copies to make the $1000.

> Book A (Traditional publisher): 2000 units sold to make $1000.
> Book B (Self-publish): 250 units sold to make $1000.

Neat bit of math! Makes the self-publishing option look good. But be careful. Go back and re-read all the previous; self-publishing is a tough business, and make no mistake, it IS a business.

ADVANTAGES OF SELF-PUBLISHING

In spite of pointing out all the negatives of self-publishing, it does have advantages.

Timely. If something must be in print quickly, you can't beat self-publishing, which can put a book in print within a couple weeks.

More Profit. As the math showed above, you can make more profit on fewer sales with a self-published book. For micro-niche markets, it may be the right choice.

Control. Okay. If control is really your issue, then self-publish.

RESOURCES ON SELF-PUBLISHING

I can't convince you NOT to self publish? Then at least do yourself a favor and read more about the business. On my blog at IndieKidsBooks.com, I talk about the self-publishing business for children's books. Or see my publishing house website at MimsHouse.com—and buy a couple books!

ACTION POINTS

Assess your skills at writing, graphic design, marketing, your ability to build a platform, etc. Or, will you be able to afford freelance help in those areas? After an honest look, do you still think you're cut out for the self-publishing market? If so, come join me at IndieKidsBooks.com

THE BIGGEST MISTAKE IN SUBMITTING

Assuming you want to traditionally publish your book, what is the biggest mistake made when submitting a picture book to a publisher?

YOU DO NOT NEED TO FIND AN ILLUSTRATOR

The most frequent question I get is this: "How do I find an illustrator for my book?"

You don't. The publisher chooses the illustrator.

In fact, you cut your chances of selling in half if you try to team up with an illustrator and submit a package. The editor may love the text, but not the art; or, love the art, but not the text. Either way, you get a "no." Reputable trade publishers do not want you to find an illustrator, or pay for an illustrator, or do anything more than provide illustration possibilities in your text.

After editors decide to publish your picture book, they decide on likely illustrators by looking at factors like these:

Style. What sort of style seems best for this story? Watercolor v. pastels? Modern v. traditional? Perhaps collage?

Reputation. Who is up and coming? What illustrator is building a reputation and could add to the sales potential of this story? Or, is there a new illustrator they'd like to take a chance on?

Track Record. Who have they worked with before? Does the illustrator deliver on time? Does the illustrator do good research for the type story; i.e. for a historical, does the illustrator research clothing styles, etc.?

LIKE YOU, THE PUBLISHER WANTS TO SELL BOOKS

Always, the publisher is looking for ways to improve sales of your book by matching it with the best illustrator. Once the editor and art director agree on an illustrator, and the illustrator accepts the project, the publisher takes care of the contract and any money that will change hands. You sit back and wait.

DO YOU HAVE INPUT INTO THE CHOICE OF AN ILLUSTRATOR?

The level of your input depends on the editor and art director involved. Once, an editor asked me to look at several illustrators and kept me in the loop as the text was sent to a couple possible illustrators. At a different publisher, the editor kept things close to the chest and told me nothing until the illustrator signed a contract.

You can usually, however, suggest illustrators, and an editor will always be glad to review a professional portfolio. That means your neighbor is out, unless s/he has a professional portfolio.

But what if you want to work with your neighbor? Sell your text first. Then, ask the editor to consider a portfolio, dummy book, or sample illustrations. That way, you keep a friend, but still sell your text.

ACTION POINTS

If you have an illustrator in mind, check to see if s/he has a professional portfolio to present to an editor or art director. When your story is accepted, be ready to ask the editor if they will look at the portfolio, but be ready for the editor to say no, they already have someone in mind.

ILLUSTRATORS DON'T TELL YOU WHAT TO DO

The illustrator doesn't tell YOU what to do, so don't tell the illustrator what to do!

PROFESSIONAL RESPECT

You do your professional job with the text and the illustrator does his/her professional job with the art. Respect is the key here.

If you want to dictate some of the art to the illustrator, please put it in the text. Otherwise, let the illustrator choose.

NOTES TO ILLUSTRATOR: WHEN? WHY?

Is there any time you can send a note to the illustrator? Yes. When the text and art must conflict someway. For example, in Katy Duffield's picture book, *Farmer McPeeper and the Missing Milk Cows*, the almost-blind-farmer-because-the-cows-stole-his-glasses keeps making statements about what he sees, and he's wrong. The story's humor comes partly from the disconnect between what Farmer McPeeper sees and what the reader sees—we know he's wrong!

In this type story, you do need to provide notes to the illustrator. But really, you don't need much and maybe even just a note in the cover letter could be enough: "Because Farmer McPeeper is virtually blind without his glasses, he won't understand that he's really seeing the cows as they cavort and play." Then, let the illustrator take it from there. Usually, you don't need illustrator notes.

WHAT IF YOU HATE THE ART? GET BEHIND THE BOOK!

If there's a mistake in the artwork, point it out to the editor immediately and they will ask the illustrator to correct it. My picture book, *Searching for Oliver K. Woodman*, was a sequel to *The Journey of Oliver K. Woodman*, so the details had to be consistent between books. The illustrator, Joe Cepeda, accidentally changed a character from left-handed to right-handed; when it was pointed out, he immediately made the change.

If the art is simply—in your opinion—awful, you can talk to the editor and ask them to reject the art or ask for it to be redone. But, most contracts don't give you veto power, and you must accept the editor's opinion. Consider carefully if you want to have this discussion with the editor because it could affect other dealings with the editor and publisher.

In the end, you must find a way to reconcile yourself to the illustrator's vision. You can't go around trashing the art because that means you are trashing YOUR BOOK! You should resolve to never mention it outside your family, and then, get behind the book and help promote it.

Let me reassure you: this rarely happens. When I receive the final copy of a book, it's the death of one book—the one in my head—and the birth of a new book that is what the illustrator saw in his or her head. Always, it's been a better book than I could ever have imagined. I trust illustrators to take my words and turn them into something magical. You should trust them, too.

ACTION POINTS

Write notes to the illustrator for your manuscript. Then, try to put everything absolutely necessary into the text itself. Read it over: do you really need that note to the illustrator to make the story work? Try to do without it unless the art should contradict something in the text.

TITLES AND SUBTITLES SELL YOUR WORK

Titles are essentially a marketing tool that will help you sell to readers.

APPEAL TO TWO AUDIENCES

Picture book titles must catch the interest of both parents and children. It's hard to keep in mind and harder to pull off, but you must appeal to both levels of readers. Parents want something snappy and memorable, while kids like something with language play. Titles are sales tools, and as such, you should take time to find the right title.

PHYSICAL SIZE

Make sure the title will fit on the spine of the book. I've suggested really long, fun titles, only to be pulled back to reality by the physical book in hand.

BRAINSTORMING TITLES

You spent time earlier developing a working title. Go back to your list of possible titles and reevaluate. Research for any similar title already in print and try not to repeat a title. Titles aren't copyrightable, but you still don't want to create reader confusion. Be ready to suggest several titles to the editor and the publicity team. Ultimately, the title is the publisher's decision. If you self-publish, you are the publisher, so you'll decide.

EFFECTIVE PICTURE BOOK SUBTITLES

Do you have to include a subtitle? Well, no, not strictly. Just like any other book, a subtitle is a chance to tell the prospective reader something more about the topic of the book. For picture book biographies, titles are often some provocative phrase, followed by the person's name, and this feels very natural. For example, Susanna Reich's picture book is titled and subtitled, *Jose! Born to Dance: The Jose Limon Story*.

While a subtitle isn't necessary, you may want to use one because those extra words can make your book easier to find online and in databases. Consider including key words in your titles. For example, if I were to add a subtitle to my picture book, *19 Girls and Me*, it would be "Kindergarten Friendships" or even, "Back-to-School Kindergarten Friendships between Genders." I don't want that clunky subtitle on the book anywhere! I just want it included in databases to make it easy to find for categories that teachers might search. And they will search "kindergarten friendships." Maybe they won't search "gender friendships." Unless it's Women's History month. But maybe they will.

Talk to your editor about using a subtitle just for databases. It's not a common practice yet, but it makes perfect sense.

ACTION POINTS

What are your favorite picture book titles?

Write subtitles for some of your favorite books, trying to think about how it would be found in a search engine.

Decide on a title and subtitle for your story. However, keep several other favorite options at hand for discussion with your editor.

HOW DO YOU FIND AN EDITOR'S NAME?

You know that it is important to list the name of the submissions editor on any submission package; however, you're having a hard time finding the name of a specific editor. Should you try to find a specific editor's name for submission, or just send to "Dear Submissions Editor?"

Never send to just a "Submissions Editor"! Dig deeper!

You research until you find someone specific.

Editorial Director Arthur Levine, Arthur Levine Books, Scholastic once said that finding the right editor is like finding a great sweater. If he only likes pullover sweaters, then it doesn't matter how great the style of a button up sweater, he won't buy it. Each editor has genre preferences, quirky things they dislike, and so on. You need to find the right person for your story, not just an editor's name. As you look for information on editors, look also for their tastes in literature.

INTERNET SEARCH

Do a basic search of a publisher as a starting point. Do specific searches for an editor's name, for example, "NameofPublishingCompany Editor." You can often find an editor's blogs or social media accounts. FOLLOW some editors for a while to understand their interests and passions.

Study the current lists of a publisher and a specific imprint: Does your manuscript fit what they publish?

Look for lists of editor interviews.

Research events that connect writers and editors. The Rutgers One on One Plus conference has a nice list of editors at publishing houses. Besides attending a conference like this, you could use the list to research each editor. Go for assistant editors who are young and hungry to build their own list of authors. The senior editors already have a list of people they work with, and it's harder to get in and the bar is higher.

USE ORGANIZATION RESOURCES

The SCBWI (www.scbwi.org) is the Society of Children's Bookwriters & Illustrators, the only professional organization dedicated to those who write and illustrate for children. There are many local chapters and lots of help available. Check the scbwi.org pages for possible conferences where you can meet some of your favorite editors.

NETWORK

The SCBWI (open for members only) has a bulletin board for discussions on many topics. One category lists editors and agents, and also their response times, or the amount of time it takes for him or her to reply to various submissions.

Network. Find happy writers and ask about their editors.

Attend conferences and meet editors. After listening to a presentation, you'll have a better idea of whether or not this editor would like your work. In other words, you still need to make that personal connection! It's a personal business and you'll sell better if you've met someone.

ACTION POINTS

Find the names of 5-10 editors who are likely to buy your manuscript.

RESOURCES

Here, you'll find resources to help you learn to write and sell your children's picture book.

ORGANIZATIONS

Children's Book Council (cbcbooks.org)
The CBC sponsors Children's Book Week and Children's Poetry Week. They have an online listing of member publishers and how to contact them.

Society of Children's Bookwriters and Illustrators (scbwi.org)
The SCBWI is the professional organization for those writing and illustrating for kids. Each state has a regional coordinator, and contact information is on the website.

PUBLICATIONS

Children's Writers and Illustrator's Market (Always get the current year, which is usually available in late fall.)
This annual market guide lists publishers, names of editors, contact information, needs, etc. for book and magazine publishers. The book is published in late fall, so be sure to get the updated version.

Horn Book Magazine (www.hbook.com)
This magazine offers articles about children's literature, including full-text of acceptance speeches for major awards such as the Newbery and

Caldecott. Articles cover a wide variety of topics, and reviews of major new books is a good way to keep up to date on this rapidly changing field.

WEBSITES

The Purple Crayon (www.underdown.org)
Maintained by Harold Underdown, author of *The Idiot's Guide to Publishing Children's Books*, this page keeps track of which editors are moving where. His website has great up-to-date information on the industry.

Publisher's Marketplace (www.publishersmarketplace.com)
PM has a free Daily Lunch email that keeps you up-to-date on publishing news. Paid members can receive the Deluxe Lunch, which includes more articles and more in-depth coverage. You'll also get access to their Deals database and can search agents, editors and publishers to see who is buying what.

Darcy Pattison (darcypattison.com, Mims House.com and IndieKids-Books.com)
My website, Fiction Notes, discusses writing novels and picture books, and has many archived articles. MimsHouse.com is my indie-publishing company. IndieKidsBooks.com focuses on the business of indie publishing for kids.

LIBRARIES

Library Cards are Gold. To write great picture books, read 100 picture books that have been published within the last 5 years. Really. 100. Or 200. I try to take a month and do this once a year, at least. You need to know what current books are like.

Also, be sure to take advantage of your local library's ability to borrow books from other regional libraries through the inter-library loan program. This can often save you time and money.

SELF-PUBLISHING RESOURCES

If you are interested in self-publishing your picture book, it's a hard road to go: you must do all your own marketing, and unless you're famous, you won't sell many books. I can't dissuade you? Then, join me at IndieKidsBooks.com.

WORKBOOK

In this section, you'll find helpful worksheets. Use these as you plan and write your picture book.

PLAN YOUR TOPIC

Plan Your Topic: Write your general idea here.

What is the overarching idea or theme in your story idea? How can you strengthen this theme in your choice of characters, setting and plot?

Characters:

Setting:

Plot:

PLAN YOUR CHARACTERS

Name of Protagonist or Main Character:

Description

Background

Characteristics

How does the character change over the course of the story?
i.e. from selfishness to kindness. This change must happen gradually over the course of the story.

Name of Antagonist Character:

Description

Background

Characteristics

How does the character change over the course of the story? (The antagonist may not change.)

Name of Supporting Character:

Description

Background

Characteristics

How does the character change over the course of the story? (Supporting characters may not change.)

Name of Supporting Character #2:

Description

Background

Characteristics

How does the character change over the course of the story? (Supporting characters may not change.)

PLAN YOUR SETTING

Where will the story take place? Include time of year, time of day, geographic location, location within a house or school, etc. Usually a story moves from place to place, so you'll need several settings. For each setting create a word bank of sensory images. When you write don't try to include them all. Instead include the important details.

Setting #1: Mood Sensory Details   Mood_____

Name the overall mood of this setting. Then choose details to support that mood.

See?

Hear?

Smell?

Touch (not emotions; think temperature and texture)?

Taste?

If you zoom out to a panorama, what do you see, hear, smell, touch, taste?

If you zoom in close, what do you see, hear, smell, touch, taste?

Setting #2: Mood Sensory Details   Mood_____

See?

Hear?

Smell?

Touch (not emotions; think temperature and texture)?

Taste?

If you zoom out to a panorama, what do you see, hear, smell, touch, taste?

If you zoom in close, what do you see, hear, smell, touch, taste?

THUMBNAIL LAYOUT
FOR A 32-PAGE PICTURE BOOK

16	17

	1

18	19

2	3

20	21

4	5

22	23

6	7

24	25

8	9

26	27

10	11

28	29

12	13

30	31

14	15

32	

PLOT SUMMARY - THIS IS A STORY ABOUT. . .

For a cause-effect plot structure, fill-in-the-blanks.

This is a story about _____

who more than anything else wants _____

but can't because

1) _____

2) _____

3) _____
(Optional: repeat as many times as your story demands.)

until _____.

EXPLORE YOUR OPTIONS

Explore the WAY you tell the story by looking at the point of view, storytelling options and setting. By doing short explorations of these options, you may find a better voice, a more intriguing and unusual option, or simply something you like better. To use, try starting your story from each variable.

EXPLORE POINT OF VIEW OPTIONS

Narrative voice :

1st person

2nd person (Direct Address, or Talking to the Reader)

3rd person

Change the POV character

Apostrophe (speak to the inanimate)

EXPLORE STORYTELLING OPTIONS

Straight narrative - chronological

Letters or Diary

Folktale

Poetry or Ballad

EXPLORE SETTING OPTIONS
Exotic

Familiar

Change time period (future, past, invented)

Different location (Africa or Antartica; park or back yard; pig pen or barn; etc.)

OTHER EXPLORATIONS
Combine several of the elements above and try starting a draft of your story with a unique combination of options.

REVISE IN 7 WAYS

Revision of your picture book manuscript can go through many stages. Here are the main ways I look at revising. Use this as a guide to the stages of revising.

Narrative Arc
    Beginning
    Middle
    End
    Page 32

Length - Cut in Half
    Microcuts

Mentor Texts -
    Pastiche
    Word Play

Page Turns & Interactive

Voice
    Phonics
    Sentence Variety

Dummy
    Evaluate each page, pacing, read aloud qualities, etc.

Does this story need a Quantum Leap Revision?
    You've worked with this draft for over a year.
    New information.
    New skills from a class.

OTHER WRITER RESOURCE BOOKS BY DARCY PATTISON

http://mimshouse.com/product-category/write/

Made in the USA
Coppell, TX
22 May 2020